GOD
IF YOU ARE REAL
SHOW ME!

MICHELLE LEA

God! If You Are Real, Show Me!

S.H.E. PUBLISHING, LLC

SHE PUBLISHING LLC

For information contact:

Email: info@shepublishingllc.com
Website: www.shepublishingllc.com
MUNSTER, INDIANA | INDIANAPOLIS, INDIANA
Library of Congress Control Number: Forthcoming

ISBN: 978-1-964061-39-9

First Edition: October 2025

10 9 8 7 6 5 4 3 2 1

Dedications

I thank God for blessing me with many gifts and talents and I dedicate this memoir to the following special people:

- To my mom, Rita Callahan – I thank God for my mom, a very strong and supportive woman who always supported my gifts.
- To my dad, R. B. Callahan, who was an example of how a man supports his family and my dreams.
- To my daughter, Larita. I'm very proud of how she turned her life around to become an example in youth counseling. She is also an example for others who struggle through addiction and loss. To her husband, Lennard, who's been a great support to his wife and family and to me, also.
- To every pastor that made a great impact on my life.
- To my graphic designer, Michelle Hudson, fondly known as Chelly. She was able to design what I described into a perfect book cover.
- To Donna Ridge, who enthusiastically took on my project with her typing and editing skills.
- To Shenitha Burton, CEO of S.H.E. Publishing for taking on my memoir and personally working beside me with it.

Table of Contents

Foreword

This is a journal of a purpose-filled life.

All the chapters are real. They are true accounts of my family as we grew over the years. Many of these chapters were written many years ago. I pondered the accounts in my heart – sharing first with my children – many accounts they actually lived through. I share with others, especially those who don't know God, and to those who were raised as I was, with no church affiliation – just house rules.

Nowadays, you don't hear much about what God has done and very little to none of what I shared in this book. After I was put in challenging situations, I challenged God. I didn't believe God could or would hear or even answer my prayers – not to mention the unspoken prayers of my heart's desires.

I was very curious as a child. My constant thoughts were what caused the wind, trees, lakes and timed occurrences such as the sun and moon? I asked who or what controls this? I was forced to ask God – "If you are real, show me!"

The Potter's House

Jeremiah 18:1-4:

> *The word that came to Jeremiah from the Lord, saying, "Arise and go down to the potter's house, and there I will announce My words to you." So I went down to the potter's house, and there he was, making something on the wheel. But the vessel that he was making of clay was spoiled in the hand of the potter; so he remade it into another vessel, as it pleased the potter to make. (NASB)*

I had read these words over the years, but one day when I read these words, God had me hear the words. These words took me back to high school. At this time, I did not know God as Lord and Savior -- Master of my Soul.

I joined a pottery class to get that easy 'A' in Art. I thought it would be fun to get an 'A', but to my dismay, I was wrong. I really wanted to run after the teacher passed around bricks of clay in clear cellophane. Well, I discovered it was too late in the semester to run. There are many times when we run into bumps in the road -- I had to see it through.

We were given this hard brick of clay. We were instructed to unwrap and soften it. I twisted it, broke it, and smashed it -- all in the impossible attempt to soften it. I guess this must be how God sees us when working on us – hard as an unfinished lump of clay. It took all my strength, yet it wasn't ready for the potter's wheel. We were told to work it thoroughly to soften to ensure there were no bubbles. It really sounded like simple enough instructions. Absolutely not! This fun easy-A class became so stressful and difficult. I even tried kneading it like dough. It seemed to help or make it more difficult. At this point, I really wanted to quit.

I looked back on this experience, thinking how many times I have been faced with any challenges. Now I see it as difficult and impossible to attain. Now you begin to rethink the task wanting to quit while thinking -- this must not be for me. If there was a God, He would've strengthened me through it. Well, not necessarily! I realized the more difficult the task, the greater the lesson and the greater the reward. Of course, many of us don't see this until it's over. Hindsight is definitely 20/20.

Hebrews 10:35-36:

Therefore, do not throw away your confidence, which has a great reward. For you have need of endurance, so that when you have done the will of God, you may receive what was promised. (NASB)

With my lack of patience and against the instructions given, I proceeded to put this unprepared lump of clay on the pottery wheel. I decided to add water to further soften it (a step that was for prepared clay, after working out all the bubbles.) So, I took a bit of a short cut. There are no shortcuts in God, at least none worth achieving. I continued forming my vase, looking around at the other tables and all the busy hands, with expressions of difficulty and envy when looking at me. I could only think how amazing it felt – watching my fingers as I wet my hands in water, as I was shaping the vase watching my fingers now the color of the clay. While changing the shape, I briefly took my eyes off the wheel, looking around at others just putting theirs on the wheel, while many were still pounding, mine suddenly collapsed. I should've kept my eyes on the prize!

I've learned so many lessons from this experience. I completed my vase the following day. I was ready to paint – it dried overnight. Many in the class were still working their clay. I was so excited – mine now painted bright cheery colors. The teacher would put them in the kiln (pottery oven).

I couldn't get there fast enough the next day to see my beautiful vase and take it home. I was the first in the class. The teacher was writing on the blackboard while I frantically looked for my vase. "Miss ----," I said. Before I could say her name, she said, "It's in the box on the back table." When I looked in the box, it was all my beautiful colors – but in many pieces!

"What happened?" I yelled out. "Did someone drop it?"

She explained, "You know we talked about how there are no shortcuts or fast finishes. If that clay is not worked thoroughly, making sure there are not bubbles in the clay before creating your masterpiece before it goes into the kiln – it will explode. Remember this, a masterpiece is not quickly created."

When I first read that scripture (Jeremiah 18), this experience flooded my mind and tied these two together. First, He told him to hear His words, meaning have a conscious understanding of what was said. *"Go where I send you."* Know that what God says is only for your good. He caused something to happen on the wheel, where no change took place. It was not the same. When God takes hold of us, or shall I say, when we surrender ourselves to God, when we allow God to take us in His hand and onto the potter's wheel, there would be a significant change that takes place in our thought processes. We see things differently.

Isaiah 64:8:

But now, O Lord, thou art our father; we are the clay, and thou our potter; and we all are the work of thy hand. (KJV)

Romans 9:20-21:

> *On the contrary, who are you, you foolish person, who answers back to God? The thing molded will not say to the molder, "Why did you make me like this," will it? Or does the potter not have a right over the clay, to make from the same lump one object for honorable use, and another for common use? (NASB)*

"In the beginning," God said of all he made *"and it was very good"* Genesis 1:31. Although we are in this world but not of this world. We are flesh, though in God's hands the vessel can be marred, in sickness, hardship, troubles.

Jeremiah 18:4:

> *The vessel that He made was marred. (KJV)*

It was flawed, disfigured, damaged, spoiled, and un-useful. It was a part of the mindset of this world *"I want it now!"* Quick, fast and in a hurry!' But lacking one most important fruit – patience (Galatians 5:22). God will use situations in our lives to mold, make and shape us, His children, on the inside. God is a loving Father of whom we can trust.

Proverbs 3:5-6:

> *Trust in the Lord with all your heart*
> *And do not lean on your own understanding.*
> *In all your ways acknowledge Him,*
> *And He will make your paths straight. (NASB)*

We must trust God who created us. He knows our path that we should take. The vessel He created in us, was to be used for His pleasure and purpose. He put everything in us that's needed to do His will and work in His vineyard. We must seek God fully to be positioned to follow the journey for our lives.

The Word of Truth (The Bible) is a road map for us from creation made by God's hands from the shaping of our souls to returning to the dust in which we came. Times may come when we allow the troubles of life to take hold of us. We become marred and in need of going back to the potter's house to be put back on the potter's wheel taking heed to God's word.

So, I went back to the potter's house (my art class). I took heed of the instructions to take my time. I did the work. This time I was able to showcase a beautiful vase made by my hands.

Second Chance

Starting with Philippians 4:19:

And my God shall supply all your needs according to His riches in glory in Christ Jesus. (NKJV)

Experiencing many encounters with God, showing me His attributes, standing behind His Word, there were wants, but more needs.

Thinking what was a single mother to do with minimal finances and two children – you pray! *God is your present help in time of trouble.* God is well aware of what we stand in need of.

Both children were born with club feet which I noticed in early infancy. My son had this condition in one foot which was corrected in only four weeks with a full cast, from top thigh to toe. In the late 70's, I removed the cast myself, using pliers after sitting him in the baby chair soaking in the bathtub.

In the early 80's, my daughter came along. She was born with this condition in both feet. Her condition was more severe than my son's. They took off one cast only to replace with another one. Her entire leg and foot were encased in plaster for four months longer than her brother's. I was happy that she was a small baby. The cast on both legs seemed to double her weight. Each doctor visit ended with each cast being removed by the doctor with an amazing saw designed to cut the boot but not the flesh!? I couldn't see how that was possible, so he assured me by turning it on, then asking for my hand – it stopped. This calmed my fears of her being cut.

When this season was over, I was given a prescription for reversed last shoes. These are shoes which appear to be on the wrong feet. Ironically, those were the shoes that she learned to walk in. But her first attempts was in her crib with casts on both legs holding onto the bars. Once the casts were removed from both legs, then another season of reversed lasts for sleeping were prescribed. These were reversed last shoes with a bar between them to further correct her feet.

I felt the real challenge was ahead. When the doctor informed me that they both had to wear Buster Brown shoes to ensure the continued correction and healing of their feet, I knew those shoes were expensive. They were both blessed to wear those shoes when needed. Unfortunately, my daughter was not able to catch her brother's shoes when they became too small for him. He had wide feet as well as a high instep. Her feet were narrow.

My Mom, who had helped her family as well as others, was not able to help me at this time. We prayed to no avail. I had three dollars, which clearly was not enough to purchase the shoes needed. I'd prayed, trusting God – knowing He has done the impossible before.

Then Mark 11:24 came to my mind:

> *Therefore I say unto you, what things soever ye desire, when ye pray believe that ye receive them and ye shall have them. (KJV)*

After prayer I felt empowered and so encouraged that I shall have the shoes I desired. Besides, all I was asking for was navy-blue Buster Brown shoes in size 2 in excellent condition.

I was so excited when my mom returned home. I asked if she could take me to a thrift store in the far south suburbs on Halsted Street. It was the route and store that came to mind in prayer. I just knew they would be there as we drove to the place I was led to go. I felt some apprehension that I was so excited to be going and for pumping up my mom about what God had prepared for me.

Walking in the store with much anticipation and expectation, I walked right to the shoe section but began to feel dismay. There was nothing even close to what I was looking for. I was so sure this was the place I saw for me to go, so I continued to look on the top shelves, hoping someone put them down somewhere else.

I returned to the car empty-handed and discouraged, yet hopeful and praying, Mom saw I had nothing. She never said a word. I continued asking God for direction, I was so sure of the route that I was instructed to go. She said nothing while taking us back home on the same path. Discouragement began to speak to me, asking where did you think you'd find those exact shoes? I began rebuking the words spoken to me. All the while as she drove, I looked at every store, shop, house and garage we passed dropping my head with eyes closed in quick prayer, asking God – I know I heard your directions so clearly. What am I missing?

I then heard, "Watch and pray." I held my head up, praying and continuing to watch every store window. Suddenly, I saw a sign extended over a store window – "Second Chance." Repeating that out loud as I read it, I yelled, "Mom, stop!" I pointed ahead at the sign which simply said, "Second Chance Thrift Store." Instantly my excitement and hope returned. I was yelling, while laughing, for Momma to stop.

I had $3.00 crumpled in my sweaty hand. I jumped out of the car with great expectations and ran in – startling the store clerk. The clerk stood behind the table displaying several pairs of shoes. She looked at me strangely, taking a step back and asked, "Can I help you?" My eyes were fixed at shoes on the display table. I was so amazed I couldn't speak, as I stared at a seemingly new pair of navy-blue Buster Brown shoes. The clerk watched me as I reached for the navy-blue shoes. I turned them over to see the size and price. Instantly, my eyes filled with tears to see that size 2 for $3.00!

I was asked by the clerk, "Will you be taking these?"

I answered, "Yes", giving them to her.

As she walked to the register, I followed her. At the register she said, "That'll be $3.08." Three dollars was all I had. I told her to let me go to the car to get the eight cents. I'm running to the car like the shoes would suddenly disappear.

"Mom, do you have eight cents?"

"No, I have nothing," she said.

I looked on the floor – back and front. Wow, I thought, not one penny! I went back in with only three dollars in my hand. The saleslady must've seen me through the glass doors as I searched for the eight cents. Walking towards her, I watched her put the shoes in a plastic bag. She handed them to me as I told her I didn't have eight cents. She said, "That's okay, this is my store." As tears ran down my cheek, I thanked her as I handed her three dollars. I asked if I could hug her. She hugged me with tears also in her eyes. I was praising God and asking for blessings for the saleslady as I walked back to the car. I took the shoes out of the bag to show my mom my blessings from the Lord.

Red Socks

JEHOVAH JIREH - THE LORD WHO PROVIDES.

Philippians 4:19: *But my God will supply all your needs according to His riches in glory in Christ Jesus. (KJV)*

Psalms 34:10: *The young lions suffer want and hunger; but those who seek the Lord lack no good thing. (RSV)*

Thinking of times when the kids were younger, my sister-in-law gave me a very pretty multicolored sundress for my Baby Girl. The top of the dress was red with white lace ruffles on each side down the front. The bottom was white with multicolored large polka dots. I could see that dress etched in my mind. Thinking what color socks would be best for this pretty dress – it came to me. Red socks with white ruffles or lace. Oooh, I thought that would be so pretty. Then it came to me, as if I were dreaming – where would I get money for such things? I did not believe in praying and asking God for such frivolous things. I cast it out of my mind, so I didn't spend a lot of time thinking of what I couldn't have. But it was still in the back of my mind.

A few weeks later, early one evening, I drove to their dad's home to pick up the kids. I blew the horn to let him know I was there. While waiting, I was singing along with the radio and tapping the steering wheel when I noticed something red in the curb on the street in front of me. I got out of the car for a closer look. There was no one in sight. In total disbelief, I bent down to pick it up.

"Oh, my God," I cried out.

It was a brand-new pair of red socks with white lace folded over with a thin piece of cord connecting the socks – and in her size! They were clean as if they were just lying there for me. I cried out in total praise to God while looking at the socks several times as if they were not real. I thanked God repeatedly because I did not ask Him for those socks.

Psalms 37:3-5:

> *³ Trust in the Lord, and do good; so shalt thou dwell in the land, and verily thou shalt be fed.*

> *⁴ Delight thyself also in the Lord: and he shall give thee the desires of thine heart.*

> *⁵ Commit thy way unto the Lord; trust also in him; and he shall bring it to pass. (KJV)*

This was not the only mysterious gift from God. I remember when my husband and I separated. My two children and I went to my mom's house. I came there with the mindset of soon moving out into our own place. Every day I'd look in the paper seeking rental apartments. My sister had the paper delivered daily. After a few months I found a one-bedroom garden apartment in Harvey. Then I learned that "garden apartment" was a fancy way of saying, "basement apartment." The rent was only $275.00.

When I came to stay with my mom, I asked my husband for $300.00 per month for child support which he gave me. From the time I stayed with my mom, I saved up for my apartment and the truck I would need to move.

My mom began asking questions. "How are you supposed to live on $25.00 a month?"

"That is not my concern, it's God's." I simply told her.

God's word says, *"God will supply all my needs according to His riches in glory by Christ Jesus."*

I'm standing on it – if God said it, I'm waiting for Him to show me by doing it. At this point, I was still challenging God. Deep down, I did not believe because I had prayed for so many things for so long. Even down to saving my husband as I lived a godly life in his presence at all times. I put blessed oil in laundry soap, mopping soap, and dish soap. Also, I prayed for God to save him. But my prayer changed after a while. I asked God to draw him in or drive him away according to His will. Then my husband gave me an ultimatum, "Either you stop going and taking my kids to that cult (church) or I'm gone." And he left!

He demanded the landlord to break the rent-to-own contract, so we had to move in one day. I didn't know. So here I am suddenly a single mother with two small children (a two-year-old and a four-year-old).

Now the test was on. I stood on the side of continuing to serve Christ. I put myself all the way out there saying if He is real, well I'm all in. And I told God that if my children are ever without their natural needs, if they ever missed meals, if they ever go hungry, I am going back to my husband and never looking back. It was hard watching my children lack daily needs.

My mom said we could stay with her, with my brother and sister. Neither mom nor siblings were believers. But growing up, my mom, who grew up in holiness, was in a backslidden state for over thirty years. As a child, we didn't attend church. My dad grew up in a Christian home, as well. His dad was a minister. Mom taught us five children the Lord's Prayer and the Golden Rule. She taught us to do unto others as you would have them do unto you. As small children, we were taught this prayer from

Matthew 6:9-13:

> *After this manner therefore pray ye: Our Father*
> *which art in heaven, Hallowed be thy name. Thy*
> *kingdom come, Thy will be done in earth, as it is*
> *in heaven. Give us this day our daily bread. And*
> *forgive us our debts, as we forgive our debtors.*
> *And lead us not into temptation, but deliver us*
> *from evil: For thine is the kingdom, and the*
> *power, and the glory, for ever. Amen. (KJV)*

I am so grateful to my mom. She was very supportive of my new way of life. Whenever I came home from church, I was excited about all the new things I learned about God and His works. She literally lived her church life through me. When the kids were in church programs, she'd be right there in full support.

One week before Easter, all the movies were centered around Jesus. "The Ten Commandments," "Jesus of Nazareth," the list went on and on about Jesus' work, His birth, death and resurrection. I didn't miss them, and I had my kids watch, as well. I was hoping they were able to get a clear understanding – because clearly, I did not. I often struggled with the fact that all Jesus endured was for me! I always cried watching Jesus being mistreated, beaten and nailed to the cross. I'd seen it before but always thought it was not real. I thought, who could endure this kind of brutal punishment. I remember how sad I felt when I learned this was true, that Jesus truly endured all this torture for me. I cried all the more thinking I was not worthy for Jesus to be tortured and beaten. I felt so bad then when I read the prophecy in Isaiah 53.

Here are verses 5-7:

> But he was wounded for our transgressions, he was bruised for our iniquities: the chastisement of our peace was upon him; and with his stripes we are healed. All we like sheep have gone astray; we have turned every one to his own way; and the Lord hath laid on him the iniquity of us all. He was oppressed, and he was afflicted, yet he opened not his mouth: he is brought as a lamb to the slaughter, and as a sheep before her shearers is dumb, so he openeth not his mouth. (KJV)

I really felt bad about how I went through little things. I was crying out to God. It was a very long time that I came to understand and be grateful for His sacrifice of love and commitment to his father. I finally realized that I really fell in love with Jesus for His love and bravery for me and so many others who felt they didn't deserve His beautiful sacrifice.

Every day at my mom's house I was looking to move out. I didn't want to be a burden to her, besides my kids were young and I had to teach them to be quiet, because my mom worked nights. Throughout the day while in the house, I tried to keep them quiet. So, I kept them out as much as I could.

Again, God's word came to me, Proverbs 3:5-7. I just didn't completely understand because I was fasting three days and nights every week, yet I was struggling to figure this out. Now I'm saved. I can have whatever I want. When I said it out loud, I sounded like a spoiled brat. But when I read the verses again, I realized it was according to God's will not mine. I just didn't want my kids confused in that environment where they weren't saved in the house. I explained this to my mom. She was very supportive of how I was raising my children. I really didn't see the big picture.

St. John 1:5:

> *And the light shineth in darkness and the darkness comprehended it not. (KJV)*

So, I continued on, moving yet again, to only be back there in less than a year. Different neighborhoods, different schools, but God kept them. They never failed a grade. I thank God for that. They kept close friendships with the kids around mom's house. I thank God for a bit of normalcy as my children grew and as I prayed to figure this whole thing out.

Crash Course in Faith

Heb.11:1:

Now Faith is the assurance of things hoped for, the conviction of things not seen. (NASB)

My mom was no longer a believer, although she grew up in a holiness church. She had walked away from the faith, for some reason. At this time, she only visited churches, when asked. What was so amazing about my mom, whenever I came in from church, was how she shared my excitement for just about everything that had happened during the service. I would feel like a person who has never seen God's green trees, grass, and how blue the sky was. How beautiful it was. That's how I saw God and His wondrous works.

Mom was so attentive to my excitement, my testimonies. She was so very supportive of my faith. I remember how many times her eyes filled with tears as I told her all of what God was doing. Excited was she, too, when I showed her the most recent miracle – those navy-blue shoes! She could hardly believe how new they were. The bottom was not scuffed or worn and the fact that we returned home with the shoes that we set out for – for my baby!

I didn't grow up in church but came to the Lord at 28 years old. Many times, I felt I had a crash course in faith. Strange thing was – this was very unusual for mom not to have any money or even change on her or in the car. It was as if God was saying, "I don't need your help." I started noticing that whenever there was a great need, she couldn't help. That forced me to learn to trust in God and learn His ways. He then gave me my first scripture,

Proverbs 3:5-6:

Trust in the Lord with all thine heart and lean not unto thine own understanding. In all thy ways acknowledge Him and He shall direct thy path. (KJV)

After all these years, I've looked back at God, leading my paths. There were times I took the correct path. But sometimes, I set out without clarity on the way in which to go. I went my own way, going ahead of God because I'd been there several times and found what I needed, so surely, this was where I was to go. Leaning to my own understanding yet leaving there disappointed. I repented for going as I desired by following my way. But acknowledging His will and agreeing to His way, my eyes were opened to where I was being sent.

Thank you, God Almighty. I love you.

During this time in my life, God was working with me in dreams and visions. Once I dreamed of standing on a large dark stone on tempestuous water. I was a great distance from the shore with no visual steppingstones in front of me. I turned, looking behind me. Again, no stones behind me. The water was choppy and frightening. The clouds were dark and low. There was little light. I was dry. So how did I get there on that stone on the water?

Again Proverb 3:5-6 came to my mind. Right then I heard in my spirit, *"Go forth."*

How? I thought. I was a bit shook up and nervous.

I heard again, *"Go forth!"* in a firmer tone.

With closed eyes I put forth my foot to step on the water. Before my foot touched the water, another large stone appeared. I looked behind me to see all the stones to this point, but there was not one stone behind me – only the one I was standing on. I realized that He'll make provisions for me to proceed forward because going back was not an option. I also thought that God did not intend for us to return to our old way of living. It would be like returning to our own vomit as in Proverb 26:11:

As a dog returneth to his vomit, so a fool returneth to his folly. (KJV)

What a great illustration of faith ... Thank you, God!

I was gripped with fear, but I learned if fear grips you along this faith journey, going backwards should not be seen as an option. If your focus is on God, going forward on this journey is the only way. Keep your focus on God.

Proverb 3:5 says,

Trust in the Lord with all your heart, And lean not on your own understanding. (NKJV).

Follow God and obey. This means everyday communication with Him and staying in His word.

Just a Bag of Chips

Deuteronomy 28:2

> *And all these blessings shall come upon you an overtake you, if you will obey the Lord Your God. (NASB)*

I was 27-years-old, coming to the Lord, with very little understanding of just about everything about God. I had left my home with my two young children. My son was four and my daughter was two. I was asked to choose my home, my comfort zone or take a leap of faith into the unknown which I knew very little about.

I was instructed by a spiritual leader to read Psalms 37.

Here is 37:25:

> *I have been young, and now am old; yet have I not seen the righteous forsaken, nor his seed begging bread. (KJV)*

So, I stood on this, on God's word.

I've never spoken about what we lack. It seems like begging to me; like we were trying each other out. Deep down I didn't believe it. So, if it was not so, I was returning to my husband and giving up that which seemed right to me. Considering I rarely finish what I start, somehow, I knew I was right. Besides, I didn't want to hear him say, "See I told you! I tried to tell you."

I stood stubbornly, still waiting to be proven right; that it wasn't really real. But God knew the end from the beginning. When the cabinets got low, I panicked and went to get assistance for food. I thought I should use my other avenues first. Then I could go to God saying, "I did my part seeking different agencies."

But I came up empty. I was honest about my income, which was $300 a month, furthermore, out of that $300, $275 went for rent. But they did not believe that I was only applying for food stamps! I confessed that I only had ice in my freezer. Yet, even though I shared with the worker that I only wanted to purchase food for my children, I was denied assistance.

Incredibly, before the end of the week, God opened the door for my baby to attend the Head Start program with bus service – both free. In addition, a nutritional breakfast and lunch were included. I was assured that the meals had to be freshly opened daily and whatever was left over had to go in the trash.

Many times, I was forced to volunteer at the school because my daughter would not stay there without me. I would turn to leave, but before I got to the door, with sweater or jacket in hand or upside down on her, she would run from her room towards me.

When asked, "Where are you going?"

She'd say, "With you!"

Frustrated with this daily ritual, I decided to just stay, since there was space in the classroom. I helped in the kitchen. Most of the time, there was only one other person working. The head cook welcomed me, saying they could sure use the help.

On one occasion, the head cook began venting, saying, "This is such a waste. I really hate tossing all this good food in the trash."

Out of nowhere, the head cook asks me, "Did I hear you say that you are a single mother?"

"Yes, I am," I responded.

She continued, "Now you can say 'No' if you'd like, but could you and your kids use this left-over food? Some of it is barely used. I hope I'm not offending you." "Not at all! Sure, I'll take it if it's okay."

"They won't know if I put it in the garbage or in my car – it doesn't matter. As long as it's not being used the next day for the children." She rewrapped what had to be wrapped and put it all in a garbage bag for me to take home. What she didn't know at that time was that I had nothing at home for dinner or breakfast.

Since it was Friday, it was going to be a long weekend. I remember falling on my knees when I got home – crying out to God with thanksgiving. From that point on the cabinets and fridge overflowed.

The next day, I went to the store within the gas station to buy toilet tissue. I had my youngest with me. While going down the aisle, my 2-year-old grabbed a small bag of cheese puffs off the shelf, giving it to me to buy for her. I put it back on the shelf, while explaining to her that I was not able to get them today and I'll get it the next time. She started whining. It broke my heart that I could not buy her this 25-cent bag of chips. I had just enough for the tissue.

She cried the whole walk home. I laid her down for a nap and falling on my knees I cried out like a child. I was still in that space, although God really just filled my fridge, freezer and cabinets. Just like a spoiled baby, myself – crying because I couldn't buy the 25-cent chips.

Yet God heard me asking Him, "Am I doing right by my kids?" Then a wave of thanksgiving came over my heart. I began thanking Him for what He's done and repenting for my unbelief and doubt. I ended my prayer, wiping tears off my face with my hand.

I heard someone knocking on my back door. It was the neighbor from the second floor and her son. He was holding a large bag of cheese puffs that my daughter had asked for. I was looking at it and her in disbelief.

She said, "I just got back from shopping. This was in my bag, and I don't know how it got in my bag because me and my boys don't like it."

At this time, I wanted to yell out, "My baby just asked for this!"

But I just responded, "Thank you, so much."

I gave them both a hug as they put it in my hands. They returned up the stairs and tears began to flow as I shut the door. I set the bag on the table and returned to my knees, crying out in praise to God for his wonderful works.

Psalms 107:5:

Oh that men would praise the Lord for his goodness, and for his wonderful works to the children of men! (KJV)

I faced many challenges in that apartment. And I saw God show up in many ways. I became like a baby – I feared nothing! Still, at times, I leaned on my own understanding, and I WAS WRONG EVERY TIME!

A Mother's Decision

Psalms 41:3

> *The Lord will sustain him upon his sickbed; In his illness, thou dost restore him to health. (NASB)*

At the time I gave my life to God, it was as simple as Romans 10:9-10:

> *That if you confess with your mouth Jesus as Lord, and believe in your heart that God raised Him from the dead, you will be saved; for with the heart a person believes, resulting in righteousness, and with the mouth he confesses, resulting in salvation. (NASB)*

I had learned the ways of the church. Such as, when you or the children are sick, you grab that bottle of blessed oil (olive oil prayed over and used as anointing oil).

Mark 6:13:

> *And they cast out many devils, and anointed with oil many that were sick, and healed them. (KJV)*

When I was sick, I would anoint myself and also, take a spoonful by mouth. And when the children were sick, they would bring me the blessed oil to pray for them.

When my children were eight and ten, I began having a recurring dream. It was of a young woman, possibly in her late teens. I could not see her face. In the dream she was lying on an open cart. I was pulling her like on a flatbed wagon of some sort. She was stiff and couldn't sit up. Her arms and legs were in a twisted position, so that they could not straighten out. I pulled her into the bathroom to bathe her on the cart. After bathing her, I put an adult diaper on her. This is all I would see in my dream. Looking at her body, I knew she wasn't a child, but I could never see her face. I took it to be that she was given to me in dreams to pray for her and her family. I knew this had to be hard for them all. I didn't take it personally. I've had dreams and visions during sleep and during my prayers concerning what to pray for. I didn't know anyone like that young woman.

About a year later, my daughter woke up complaining that her head and neck were hurting. Being such a drama queen, I thought she was trying to get out of going to school – as she's done many times before. I sent her to get the blessed oil and a spoon. I gave her a spoonful, anointed and prayed over her. Later, I did notice that she was moving a bit slower than normal. But she was quite the actress. I kissed them both and sent them off to school.

After lunch, the school called. She was in the nurse's office. The nurse allowed her to talk to me. She was crying, saying, "It came back. It's hard to hold my head up and my tongue is big. The kids are laughing at me. Can you come get me?"

I asked to speak to the nurse who confirmed what she was saying and asked, "Does she have any allergies?"

"She has hay fever. That's all that I know of."

I asked if someone could get her things. "I'm on my way to pick her up."

When I got to the school, she looked terrified. When we arrived home, I gave her more blessed oil, anointed her from head to toe with the oil, and put her to bed after praying for her. That was on a Tuesday. We normally fasted and prayed until 4:00 pm on Tuesdays and Fridays. We had choir rehearsal and Bible study that evening. I woke her up for dinner. She seemed better and her tongue had returned to its right size. She was also able to hold her head up. She didn't eat much. I felt she just needed a little rest. While in choir rehearsal, all the kids would play in the lower level of the church. Halfway through choir rehearsal, one of her friends came to me in the choir stand to give me a message from her. It simply said, "It's happening again." I excused myself from the choir and went downstairs. I could see her from across the room. Her eyes were slightly bulging out, and she was struggling to hold her head up. Her tongue was bigger, and her head kept falling backward. She complained of a terrible headache. I pulled her to me, holding her head to my chest praying as hard as I could. Three other mothers joined me in praying for her. The pastor's mother suggested taking her to his office to pray for her. She could barely walk. We practically carried her. When we got to his office, he yelled, "Jesus!" when he saw her. We all cried out to God to heal her. Then she fell to the floor – eyes bulged, tongue swollen, slobbering and moaning as her body began to twist. Her arms and legs stiffened. I cried out, looking at her and questioning whether I did right by her. Should I have taken her to the emergency room? I started crying for my suffering baby.

The pastor stopped rebuking the devil and told me to leave. I saw her getting worse. I stopped praying and started crying while questioning whether I should stop this and take her to the hospital. I left out of his office and sat on the top stair by his door. I got a flash of my dream of the young woman on the cart and saw her face. I cried out in sequence with the prayers in the office.

After an hour, I could hear her whimper. The door opened with the pastor carrying her still wet body. She was drenched in sweat – they all were. He carried her into the sanctuary, asking for a chair. I was already half an hour late for Bible study. Pastor cancelled Bible study class. She was forced to bend in the chair.

Pastor called out to the people in the church, saying, "If you don't believe God will heal her, please leave the altar and go to the back of the church. I only want those with faith and trust who believe in God to stay and pray." Many wanted to watch but went to the back as he asked. Her brother moved back a bit, but close, crying and praying. The kids that stayed to watch were sent to the back as well. I stayed, crying out to God for my baby's complete healing and deliverance.

At this point, it was far too late to think about going to the hospital. I knew she needed God. I had never seen anything like this before. It was a very frightening sight. She continued to moan, seemingly unable to speak. Pastor and the mothers were on the floor with her clapping and crying out to God. They were praying for Jesus to heal and deliver her – commanding that evil force to let her go. Again, I closed my eyes and questioned my actions as a mother. I was fighting to stay focused on God to heal this unrecognizable attack of the devil. My hope was in God. I knew God was able. I believed.

Then, I heard her suddenly cry out. When I opened my eyes and looked at her, she was soaking wet as if someone poured water on her and her clothes. But she looked perfect. I grabbed her, holding her close, crying out praises to God.

She looked around as if she didn't know what was happening. Her eyes, tongue, arms and legs were perfect. When pastor stood her up, I held her so tight, thanking God for giving her back to me. The time was well spent. It took the entire Bible study time, and more. She was absolutely exhausted. She was seated in a chair. I was still crying praises to God while I hugged pastor and the mothers for not giving up on my baby.

I took her home. At this time, we lived in the house adjacent to the church. Some of the members helped me get her home and upstairs. I prepared a bath for her. When I undressed her for her bath, God revealed and confirmed that it was her in my dream. Now I was wondering would that have been her fate, had I taken her to the emergency room and, no doubt – surgery? That night after putting both kids to bed, I dropped to my knees crying out praises of total gratitude and adoration to God.

James 5:14-15:

Is anyone among you sick? Let him call for the elders of the church, and let them pray over him, anointing him with oil in the name of the Lord. And the prayer of faith will save the sick, and the Lord will raise him up. And if he has committed sins, he will be forgiven. (NKJV)

Whatever that was, that God delivered her from. Seemed to have made it's exit from every pore in her body. I was so grateful to God for her healing. I wanted to know what that was that came upon her. I realized it was an awesome testimony. I felt it was very serious. I wanted to know. So, I fasted and prayed for an answer. I was told she was very sick and God healed her, and for this, I was grateful because as a mother, my mind went to "What If?"

I watched her daily because I'd never seen anything like that before. I thank God to this day that it never returned.

About four years later, my cousin asked if my daughter could come to California to take care of her children for the summer while she worked. I allowed her to go. After she was gone, my son insisted that we go to Pizza Hut. We went and I decided to eat in. All he could talk about was that Big Foot Pizza with ham and pineapples. The waitress who waited on us, a middle-aged woman, laughed when he ordered. I told her to just make half sausage. She seemed to be drawn to us. She walked away laughing, saying, "Let me put this order in."

She returned to the table with our drinks and explained why she laughed. She thought he was an only child, but I explained that his sister was in California helping my cousin for the summer.

"Do you have any children? I asked her.

"I have a daughter."

"How old is she?"

"She's 19 and away at college." Then she suddenly became sad.

"Is she okay?", I asked her.

She blurted out, "She is now."

Before I could say anything, she began telling me that her daughter had to wear a helmet because she had a metal plate in her head.

Shyly, I asked, "What happened to her?"

She began telling me how she woke up one morning. "Her eyes were bulged, she couldn't hold her head up, she complained of a really bad headache, and she couldn't speak because her tongue as swollen. My pastor lived close by, so I called for him to come."

At this point all I could think of was – Oh my God! My son looked at me. I shook my head 'no', slightly, not to say anything.

She went on to say, "When he got there, he prayed for her, but she continued to get worse. Her arms and legs were folded and she couldn't stand. He told me to call 9ll. I was so scared. When I called, they came quickly. When we got to the hospital, the doctor came out to tell me that her brain was swelling, and they had to cut part of her skull to alleviate the pressure."

I began to tear up for her baby and mine. That could have been my daughter's fate. She continued saying that her daughter was hospitalized for months. I knew this was God, answering my prayer. So, I asked her, "Did they tell you what it was that caused her brain to swell?"

She replied, "I believe the doctor said it was spinal meningitis."

"How is she now?" I asked.

"She's fine now, but started college a year late, and like I said – she still wears a helmet for protection. But she's okay. Let me get your pizza."

When she walked away, my son said, "That's the same thing that happened to my sister. Why didn't you tell her?"

"I didn't want her to feel bad," I said. That was her decision as a mother, just like it was my decision to trust God for healing. Besides, I had asked God years ago to tell me what that was that attacked her body. He just did! Thank you, Father!

When the pizza came with chunks of pineapple and ham, I laughed telling him, "Stay on your side and enjoy it."

The Blue Car

Psalms 84:11:

For the Lord God is a sun and shield; the Lord gives grace and glory; no good thing does he withhold from those who walk uprightly. (NASB)

When we lived in a pretty rural area, the busses ran only on the main streets. So, when the kids and I went to church or family's homes, we had to walk. So, one Sunday we walked to church which was four blocks away. I noticed a small used car lot on the corner in route to the church. It was about a block from my home. We walked this way at least twice a week and I had never seen this lot before. It was closed at this time, so I thought I'll go by there on Monday after taking the kids to school – and get myself a car.

After I walked the kids to school on Monday, I went to the car lot with no money, but full of faith. I didn't look long before I saw a beautiful blue Cutlass Supreme, with a white top and white leather interior. This car was so beautiful to me. I know who I am – I am God's child. He knows what I have need of.

Before leaving home, I prayed, read this scripture, wrote it down, and took it with me –

St. John 15:7:

> *If ye abide in me, and my words abide in you, ye shall ask what ye will, and it shall be done unto you. (KJV)*

At this time, my church was four blocks away, but I'd been visiting my cousin's church in Chicago on 75th and Rhodes. I was very interested in joining this church, so I really needed a car.

After walking the children to school, I went straight to the car lot. When I was crossing the street, my eyes were fixed on a beautiful blue Cutlass with a while vinyl top. I went right to it. As I was walking to the car, a salesman met me there. The first thing I asked him was, "Can I test drive it?"

He replied, "It won't start."

"What's wrong with it? I asked.

He replied, "Well, we don't know. It won't start and we jumped it – it just wouldn't start. Listen, we have another Cutlass I can show you."

"No thanks, Sir. How much is this car?"

He looked up puzzled, "I have to sell it to you 'AS IS' because we don't know what's wrong with it."

"I understand. So how much is it?"

He looked at me, then at the car and said, "Give me $300. If you can't fix it, you can't bring it back," he said repeatedly.

Ignoring what he was saying, I asked, "Can you please hold it until tomorrow?"

He said, "It'll be here."

Thanking him, I turned to walk away. I prayed the whole way home. "If that's my car, God, show me and also show me where to get the money from."

When I went to the dealership, all I had in my purse was loose change. When I got home, I read every scripture on faith and prayed again. That night I saw myself driving that car with my kids and the neighbors in my building riding with me to church.

After taking the kids to school, I called my mom, telling her about my car.

She asked, "How much is it?"

"$300."

She laughed. "What's wrong with it?"

I began explaining to her, "Hear me out. It won't start and they don't know what's wrong with it."

She laughed again, "Michelle, really!"

"But momma, I prayed about it. Last night I dreamed I was driving it to church. Besides, there can't be too much wrong with it. I didn't smell that 'old man smell' in the car."

She asked, "What does that even mean?"

"When looking for a car in the past, I've noticed the cars with a lot of issues had the smell of oil and old men, meaning they were in and out of the car a lot in the attempt to fix it."

"But you don't know how much it'll cost you to fix it," she replied.

"Momma, it can't be that much!"

"Ok, if we get this car, how will you get it fixed?" as she chuckled.

I replied, "That's not my worry."

"Then, whose worry is it?"

"It's God's and He don't worry – He just do it." She laughed again.

I asked, "Can you bring your friend so he could check out the car?" He knew about cars. She asked him. He asked, "When?"

I told her, "I told the salesman in the morning. Can you both meet me there at 10 am?"

She continued to chuckle, "We'll meet you there in the morning."

My mom's male friend came out and looked it over, telling me and mom, "It looks good – even under the hood." Without asking me how I'll get it off the lot, he gave the man a $300 check! I asked the salesman if I could pick it up the following day. I was so excited. I hugged my mom and her friend, thanking him. He told my mom, "Seems to be a good car with good tires."

The salesman had walked away. When he returned with the keys, he told me that it would be okay for the car to stay there until tomorrow. When mom pulled off after offering me a ride home, I thought that was funny seeing that I just bought a car. I walked to the pay phone – praying every step. I was asking God, how will I get the money to get the car fixed. As I prayed, my dad came to my mind. The pay phone was in the gas station about a block and a half away. I called my dad and told him the good news. "I have a car."

His response, "From where?" I told him how the car came about.

"So, what's wrong with it?" he asked.

I responded, "They don't know."

He laughed.

I told him, "I dreamed…"

He laughed again.

I spoke out during his laughter, saying, "God showed me driving. Dad, it's my car."

He stopped laughing and asked, "What's the address, so I can send a tow truck to pick it up." He told me to meet the tow truck to give them the keys at 9:30 a.m. the following day. He told me he was sending it to the Montgomery Ward Auto Shop in Evergreen Plaza in Chicago.

Later that evening, my dad called my cousin to tell me that he was coming to pick me up to go pick up my car. It was ready.

"What!!" I said. I couldn't believe that it was ready that fast. I told her, "He just picked it up this morning!"

My cousin lived a few blocks away. So many times, when my mom or dad needed to get a message to me, she would come and tell me. She didn't come in the house; she only came to give me the message. I couldn't wait until she left. I ran in the room, falling to my knees crying and thanking God for His favor and His goodness, His grace, and for being a Great Father. I was still on my knees when I heard a horn blowing. He hated blowing his horn for us. Wiping my face, I ran out the door, jumped in the car grabbing and hugging him and thanking him for his generosity. He said, "I can't wait to see this special car that you had to have so badly, that you talked your mom into buying a car that, not only wasn't running, but they had no idea what was wrong with it." He laughed. I cut into his laughing again, saying, "But now it runs. Thank you, Jesus."

When I got to the shop, the blue car was clean and shiny, with a fresh smell on the inside. My dad had them to clean it up, as well. Tears ran down my cheek uncontrollably.

He said, "It's alright. Nice car – but a Chrysler!"

I laughed because he only bought Chevys. I asked how much it cost to fix. He told me $125. I thought to myself, "That's all?! Wow, God. You are remarkable." I knew if that car was running, it was in mint condition. It would've been sold for a lot more. Not only did he get it repaired, but he also paid for the title and license plates and registration sticker. Nobody but God!

I hugged my dad again before he left. I was so emotional and choked up. I called my mom from the shop and told her I would stop by with my new car. She couldn't believe it was fixed already. She laughed again. It seemed as though the more they laughed, the more I cried. God knew how much I needed a car. When I got there, she came out to see this 'miracle,' she called it.

I explained that my dad sent a tow truck that took it to Montgomery Ward Auto Shop that morning. I told her the parts and labor were only $125, and he had it cleaned and also paid for the plates and stickers. She laughed again – shaking her head. I cried again.

She asked, "Why are you crying?"

I blurted out, "God did this! This is all God. I'm so grateful. I needed it. He did it for me. Thank you again for the part you did – making it happen for me."

God is so good. It seemed like every week or so, God was showing Himself to me, as well as to my mom. God did not hide His blessings under a bush. He blessed me openly. My siblings didn't know God, but they also saw His mighty deeds.

Psalms 150:1-2:

> *Praise ye the Lord. Praise God in his sanctuary: praise him in the firmament of his power. Praise him for his mighty acts: praise him according to his excellent greatness. (KJV)*

I prayed, 'Lord help their unbelief.' We grew up in a dysfunctional home where God was not poured into us at all. We knew the Lord's Prayer, which probably lingered from my parents' childhood.

St. Mark 9:23-24:

> *Jesus said unto him, If thou canst believe, all things are possible to him that believeth. And straightway the father of the child cried out, and said with tears, Lord, I believe; help thou mine unbelief. (KJV)*

I know that car was sent straight from heaven. I was telling all the neighbors in my building about God's goodness and of His love. They didn't have transportation, and they started coming to church with us – they and their children. Many times, there were as many as nine people in that blue car headed to 75th and Rhodes.

We all seemed to be in the same predicament – no money. I thanked God that when I got the car, my dad had me follow him to the gas station and filled it up. He also had the oil changed. When I think about all that God did through my parents, I became emotional all over again, thinking of how good God has been. I only drove when I needed to -- to save on gas. There were times when I only had 75 cents to put in the gas tank. I would pray the whole time I was pumping the gas for God to add the increase. I can honestly say I remember running out of gas only two times.

Both times I was in front of my house. I laugh as I remember taking shortcuts, also going down hills with my foot off the gas pedal in an attempt to save on gas.

The neighborhood where we lived was not the greatest. So, I didn't allow my kids to go outside except for going to the store with me. God revealed to me to take them to a park in the better neighborhood where the other parents took their children to spend time with their kids, as I did. Many times, I would take them to the forest preserves to play and I would take a sheet to cover the picnic table to have dinner. I'd bring the whole pot, with plates, forks and a jar with drinks. I sat praying while they played. They loved my spontaneous actions. I tried not to have any idle time. I didn't realize I was fighting depression. It was nothing for me to cook on a nice day, pack up the food and head to the forest preserve. I enjoyed watching them play freely. While there, they did homework, ate dinner and played. When we got home, they bathed and went right to bed. Many nights, they were asleep before their heads hit the pillow.

Sometimes, we spent the evenings taking the mothers to the store. This was a 'faith car.' Many times, I didn't have money for gas, yet I was told 'you're never home.' This was definitely a journey by faith, and God was with me every step of the way.

I always carried blessed oil (olive oil used for anointing) with me. When the car wouldn't start, I'd anoint the dashboard and steering wheel while praying a silent prayer to God. Within minutes, it would start. My gas gauge went out. So, I had no idea how much gas was in the tank. I tried to start it. It sounded like it wanted to start, but it wouldn't. We were going to church and after I put a few drops of blessed oil in the gas tank, it would start right up. I'd get back in the car, and we all sent up a thunderous praise to God. When I told people about this, they not only didn't believe it, but they told me that I was messing up my car by doing this. I didn't stop doing it. I just stopped telling the negative people. Even telling some of God's people, I could still see that spark of doubt. At this point, their doubt did not affect my faith – not one bit!

After having the blue car for months, I decided to go by the car dealership to thank them for such a great car. To my surprise, the dealership was no longer there. I pulled over to where this now vacant car lot used to be and went into a full thanksgiving praise to God that He loved me so much that He opened that car lot just for me. I shed many tears during these times. God really showed me His many attributes of love and power. There was a song on my heart:

He's sweet I know, He's sweet I know.

Dark clouds may rise, stormy winds may blow.

That I have found a savior and He's sweet I know.

I'll tell the world wherever I go

That He's sweet I know.

Again, I talked to my mom. I could see how she would take it all in. so anytime she could help me she would. But whenever she did, I'd feel so convicted. So, I shared with her that I could no longer accept her money or anything else from her.

Philippians 4:19:

And my God will supply all your needs according to His riches in glory in Christ Jesus. (NASB)

My mom continued to help, not understanding what God was doing; neither did I until I continued reading the scriptures. Then I realize God was developing and strengthening my faith in Him to not look at what man can do for me, nor my job (which I was able to work off and on due to health problems). I began to notice changes when mom insisted on helping me. I felt less of God's presence and watched my mom's finances plummet to the negative. Even when she worked overtime, she would barely have enough for herself, much less to help me or anyone else. She had a good nature to help anyone. She didn't understand but I explained to her the best I could. God wants to be my only source, yet He could touch someone to be a blessing to me.

She asked, "How do you know He didn't tell me?"

"Well, first of all" I said, "when you help me, it is like you'll get a hole in your pocket. God does not punish you for helping your child or anyone else. You are just being a mom. God knows when moms see their child suffer a need and not help them – I get it, I have children, and you help them as well. I have over twenty-five years of back learning about God and He's teaching me to depend on Him."

She then understood and stopped. It had gotten to the point where I was depending on her help. This not only hindered her livelihood but also set me back in my faith.

My car would break down with no money to get it fixed. I went back to fasting and praying three days and nights per week. Taking in no water, food, gum, nothing by mouth for the three days – that was how I was taught to fast. I knew this was how I was to get my faith back on track. I met an older man at church – turned out that he fixed cars in his garage. He ended up being my mechanic. When he fixed my car, he would ask if I would buy the part that was needed. He shared with me the junkyard where he went for parts, which was very inexpensive. Most of the time it cost me less than $40 – which included what I gave him. Although he told me I didn't have to pay him, God made sure I always had a decent amount to pay him. He was a true blessing to me. To God be the glory.

A song comes to mind when I think of the goodness of Jesus and all He's done for me. My soul cries out 'Hallelujah, thank God for saving me'. From the time I gave my heart to God,

I was given a job and a scripture. My job was to be an example –
first, in my home with my children as well as the 'onlookers' (I
call them). These are the people who watch you in all your
seasons – when things are going well and when everything seems
to fall apart. They wait for actions or reactions so they can sigh,
"Hmmm, where's your faith, where's God?" They think they
know how to live but they don't walk with God. Perhaps, they
once walked with God and fell to the wayside. They're the very
ones we need to reach.

The first scripture God gave me when I accepted Him as
Lord and Savior was

Proverbs 3:5-6:

> *Trust in the Lord with all your heart*
> *And do not lean on your own understanding.*
> *In all your ways acknowledge Him,*
> *And He will make your paths straight. (NASB)*

My life seemed complicated to me. God had me to ask
Him what to do, where to go?

I didn't come up in the church. My start came by visiting
churches with family and friends where I sat watching the people
in the church when something happened. The music changed and

got louder. The claps from the people as they stood, the claps changed to harder and louder, yelling 'Thank you, Jesus.' I thought they saw something I didn't see.

As I continued to attend, I finally understood. But when there was a shift like that, I'd cry. I didn't understand, was that God's presence and love for me? While God was working on me, He was teaching me in His word to trust Him while He helped me raise my children as a single parent. The job God gave me was not to teach as my parents taught me and my siblings, which was, 'don't do as I do, but do as I *say* do'. God wanted me to be very transparent with my children, therefore, they were told to 'do as I do *and* as I say'. I wanted them to trust and believe in God with all their heart, being set up to be blessed. I wondered why God said to do it this way, then I realized what a better way to teach them – by living life before them.

The Spirit of Addiction

Psalms 91:3

For it is he who delivers you from the snare of the trapper, and from the deadly pestilence. (NASB)

There were times when it was very difficult. I stopped smoking shortly after coming to God – alcohol and marijuana, as well. But cigarettes were my greatest challenge. I struggled with smoking because I smoked for many reasons. First, I felt it helped keep my weight down. Also, I believed it helped when stressed or upset – well, that was what I believed.

That took me back to the day I quit smoking. I remembered I would see a woman walking her child to school. I would pull over, offering her a ride. Before she walked over to the car, I'd put out my cigarette. I knew she was saved and had such a sweet humble spirit. One time, I forgot to put out the cigarette when she got in. I was so embarrassed and began apologizing while I put it out. I felt so convicted while explaining how I was saved but struggled with the cigarettes. I often prayed to stop. I never wanted my children to see me or know I was smoking. I thought, now that wasn't realistic or honest. I wanted them to go to God when they were sad, stressed or upset and not to lean towards vices, the way I did. Now the secret was out. I didn't want to be looked upon as weak or for them to start looking at me as not being very transparent. I think I should have told them about my smoking so they could see that we sometimes stumble and fall. But we could go to God for help and he would help us because no one is perfect, but our heavenly father. The Bible says He is our present help.

Psalms 46:1:

> *God is our refuge and strength, A very ready*
> *help in trouble. (NASB)*

I thought about how the life I was portraying to them may seem impossible to live. My passenger sat there listening patiently. When I finally stopped talking, she said, "I've never smoked. But my sister did, and she quit." That seemed like the hardest thing I've ever had to do. She asked if I would like her sister to help me. I excitedly said, "Yes, please, I just want to be right." She asked for my number. I hurriedly wrote my number and gave it to her.

I went back to the school to get my kids. They got out a little later. I was in a hurry to get home – I didn't want to miss that call. At this time, I was still married and we both smoked.

He didn't attend church with me and the kids. Shortly after, I put dinner on and helped the kids with homework. Her sister called. I was so happy my husband had not come home from work. I put the kids down for a quick nap before dinner.

She introduced herself as the sister of the lady I dropped off. She further explained how she once smoked and how God took the taste and desire from her. She told me how one of the sisters at church prayed for her and it left, and she had not had one cigarette or desired to smoke since that day. "Would you like me to pray for you?" she asked. I was so excited I quickly agreed. But the entire time she prayed, I was lighting one cigarette off the one before. I was just hopeless – why am I doing this? Then God's word came to me.

Romans 7:19-21:

> *For the good that I want, I do not do, but I practice the very evil that I do not want. But if I do the very thing I do not want, I am no longer the one doing it, but sin that dwells in me. I find then the principle that evil is present in me, the one who wants to do good. (NASB)*

When she was done praying, I shared with her how I was smoking the entire time she was praying. She replied, "I know but God does the deliverance." I was putting out the last cigarette

I smoked. While she finished praying, strange enough, all of a sudden, I lost the desire, I tried putting it back to my mouth, but I didn't want it at all.

"Wow!", I said out loud.

"What happened?" she asked.

I told her, "I don't want it anymore."

She began loudly praising God. It was so amazing to me –how that happened so fast. I thought it would be a process. I did not expect this to happen so fast – like instantly. I began crying, thanking God. She called out, "Michelle, do you have any cigarettes left?"

I told her, "'Bout half a pack."

She said, "OK, now throw the remaining in the garbage and profess to God and the enemy – 'I am delivered'. Say it out loud." I felt great not fighting that desire to smoke. I thanked her and continued to weep. I never heard that term before, 'I'm delivered'. I had just said and done what I was supposed to do – whatever she said. She told me, 'No problem,'" also that I can call her anytime I like if I want to pray or talk.

Unfortunately, my husband came in, saw the cigarettes in the garbage and immediately took them out, saying, "These things are too expensive to just throw away. I'll smoke them myself", even though we didn't smoke the same brand. Mine was regular and non-menthol, and his were menthol. But he did smoke mine when he was out. When he smoked his, it didn't bother me. But when he smoked mine, it really smelled bad to me. I thought it was just stale. After this, I didn't smoke for five years.

By this time, my marriage was over. It was just the kids and me. We had an apartment in Chicago. I was working with special needs adults at a training center. I loved working with them and later got a promotion to 'Behavior Specialist II.' I worked very well with them and wrote programs for them to correct behavior issues. Later, Administration asked me what school I attended, what college? I replied I didn't attend college. All I had was my GED. The director made the decision to hire me anyway. She gave me the title, and it paid a little more. She said, "Some people have God-given gifts – I take that over education. To me, it takes preference over education."

Soon, I was assigned to a 6'4" tall 16-year-old that they were having trouble with at the youth home, as well as at the workshop. But one afternoon at the workshop, one of the young men, who was somewhere in his mid-twenties, was having a problem. Another worker and I, escorted him off the work floor to an isolated room in the back, so he wouldn't set off a chain reaction and incite the rest of the clients.

First, we allowed him to get it out while telling him to calm down. Because he was a smoker, we used that to get him to calm down. He began puffing and blowing. That was how he showed us that he was trying to relax. It turned out one of the other clients took one of his pens off the table. That was the reason he was upset. In calming him, we told him we would move the other client so this wouldn't happen again. We were there with him for a little over an hour. He was very upset. That incident was very stressful. He was very aggressive. When he calmed down, he motioned for a cigarette. He was nonverbal but by this time, he was calm. I took him to the break room and when I lit a cigarette for him, I lit one for myself, as well. Immediately, I was so upset with myself, and with that one cigarette, I was re-hooked.

In our two-bedroom apartment. I would stand in the tub, lock the door, and hang partly out the window to smoke so that kids wouldn't smell it. Many times, I'd take the long way home with my jacket and a change of shirt in the trunk. I'd stop at a gas station or Walgreens to wash my face and hands, change clothes and air out the car. I sprayed the car before and after I lit up. I'd repent – always in tears.

I remember when a friend and I would take the kids out close to the lake on the side of the Science and Industry Museum to run and play – just my two and her daughter. They were close in age. While they were off playing, we'd dig a small hole to bury the cigarette in and cover with dirt if the kids were coming. I remember how I went to great lengths not to expose my weakness. At that time, I felt like I was doing the right thing. My friend was also struggling. We chose that place because it was wide and open and so beautiful. Being close to the Fieldhouse bathroom was definitely a factor with three little ones. We bought lunch, they would come and eat, then off they went to play.

Well, I felt I was doing the right thing, but truth be told, I realized I was doing something I was teaching them not to be – a hypocrite, and that saddened me. I wanted to please God. I knew at this time I was not doing my job of being an example for the kids or my friend who was watching me and struggling. I made many attempts to stop. I fasted and prayed, knowing I could not smoke during the fast. But the first thing I wanted after the fast was not food, it was a cigarette. My first attempt to quit was I stopped buying them. I started asking to borrow one. That wasn't working out either. But when I wanted one, there would be no one around. So, I started buying them again, attempting to hide the smell. I never smoked around the kids. They found out that I smoked in the past, but I quit – or so they thought. I just got better at hiding it. I just got better at deceiving them. Many smokers in the church would tell me that smoking was not a sin. But I remember hearing the scripture in 2 Corinthians 5:10:

For we must all appear before the judgment seat of Christ, so that each one may receive compensation for his deeds done through the body, in accordance with what he has done, whether good or bad. (NASB)

Seeing this scripture, I knew all the health problems I could be inviting into my Holy Vessel. But what really helped me was fear. I'd stand in the tub blowing smoke out the window when the kids were asleep and immediately after I'd repent asking God to forgive me for all my sins, for smoking. 'Help me right away,' I hear my repentant prayer repeated back to me. I heard this could happen in the scripture. This scared me so much.

Proverbs 1:25-26:

> *And you neglected all my advice*
> *And did not want my rebuke;*
> *I will also laugh at your disaster;*
> *I will mock when your dread comes. (NASB)*

I was so afraid. I heard laughter and my words spoken back to me. I knew I had to do whatever I had to do to stop. I found that my fear and love of God and not wanting to hurt Him was stronger than that nicotine craving. Hearing my words repeated back to me scared me. I felt He was done with me. I heard Big Red Gum in my spirit. I purchased a pack. Every time I'd want a cigarette, I'd chew a piece. It helped. It made my tongue feel weird and worse if I'd smoked. I did pick up a few pounds, but I didn't smoke. I first tried weaning myself off, but I found myself chewing less gum. So, I had to just quit 'cold turkey' – meaning just stop. I've heard that if you stop anything for three days, you've pretty much got it. I held on to that. I thought of the young lady who prayed for me before. I couldn't find her number. So, I prayed and confessed. I was delivered after I repented. I thank God that now lamentation after 35 years, I haven't had another cigarette. I was tempted even through all the hardships. I thank God that the smell of cigarette smoke is awful to me. I cough if around it or if I enter a room after someone smoked. That was a challenge for me. I really didn't think I was hooked because I enjoyed it. I felt it helped me with my weight and frustrations, but I found out that so did fasting – and with better benefits. I gained a closer relationship with God.

Blessings in the Valley

I was always ready and determined to leave my mom's house. But I was so blinded by my will that I couldn't see God's will. To move out was not only for the kids, but for me, as well. I remember how my mom would ask me to walk to the store to buy her cigarettes and play her lottery numbers. I told her I am not to do as she requested, but I did it to be obedient to her as my mother. My church spoke against gambling and smoking. Walking to the store and back, I found myself praying for God to save her. In the meantime, I prayed to convict her not to send me again.

I was so focused on moving out that I couldn't see what God was doing. I began to notice when she went to the store, she didn't buy cigarettes but a large bag of Skittles. She popped them in her mouth throughout the day. Wait! I thought – she hasn't been smoking or drinking except on the weekends.

An apartment came up; I moved again. Later, I found it was another premature move. So, I was back with mom again soon after moving out. Clearly, I was just running. But I couldn't see it. I was in the middle of "I'm all in God. Whatever you say, I'll do" and "I can't do that, that's not God."

I was not realizing at that time that God was moving in that house. I couldn't see what God was doing because I was walking in pride. It kept echoing in my head that I can't provide for me and my children. Then, too, I was worrying about what her friends and neighbors were saying – that I was sponging, taking advantage of my mom's generosity.

While my mind was fixed and operating in my pride, God was working in that house – right before my eyes!

I John 2:16:

> *For all that is in the world, the lust of the flesh, and the lust of the eyes, and the pride of life, is not of the Father, but is of the world. (KJV)*

I was deceiving my own self by saying I was only concerned about the kids' spirituality. But it was me – being caught up. Going back home to mom's house with my children made me feel like a failure as a mother. I never thought that God was using me and the children, too. Even the children's conversation changed to, "OOH, God's gonna get you!" They would bring me the anointing oil, if anyone was sick. I never even thought about it, but every time I returned home, God's presence was there to save and bring conviction of sins.

At last, my mind seemed to enable me to see for the first time that my mom changed before my eyes. It still brings me to tears. It was so gradual I really didn't notice.

One day after a good flesh-crucifying prayer, I realized she stopped smoking and drinking. She had already stopped cursing in front of me and my kids. I would go into her room to turn off the TV when I heard her snoring and knew she was asleep. On the TV would be Pastor Henton or Benny Hinn or the 700 Club, where they would tell many testimonies of the movement of God in the lives of the people.

I regularly prayed for my mom and siblings to come to know the goodness, righteousness and love of God. I often noticed her reading the Bible that I had given her for her birthday. She was an avid reader of many novels. But after receiving her Bible, that became the only book she would read. It didn't take her long to read it from cover to cover. Later I found that she read the Bible several times cover to cover, taking it to work and reading it on lunch and breaks.

Back at the house again, with the mind to move, I started calling apartment ads the moment I got there, without saving money. I was determined to make it work, again having our own.

The next day I was scheduled to see an apartment. I realized that my staying there was for me, as well as for the kids. Living there the kids were able to go out and play and develop life-long friendships. But then again, with all the moving and changing schools, both kids never fell behind or missed any days.

Now I realize that I am in full vanity and shame. Winter was here, and I didn't own a winter coat because the one I had the year before was no longer wearable. It didn't matter because two years prior, I was experiencing 'personal summer days', where in winter I wore a sweater coat and it was enough. But this winter, my body found its balance. Thankfully, both children had coats.

My mom saw that I didn't have a coat and gave me a coat that looked like she dug it out of the past. It was warm and it fit well. It was a multicolored tweed, three-quarter length sleeves, large buttons. I teared up when I tried it on because it fit. How very ugly, I thought, as I hugged and thanked my mom in an attempt to not offend her. With a sad heart I was about 27-years-old but felt about 70 with this coat on. I was willing to be cold rather than to wear that coat. I'd wear it to church but before entering, I'd take it off and drape it across my arm no matter how cold it was.

I was scheduled to see an apartment. Before the time to see the apartment, I was asked by one of the church mothers to take her to the grocery store. After picking her up, I began experiencing pain in my stomach. I bought some peppermints from the store – opening them right away in the store and eating several at once. I was hoping and praying that whatever it was -- this would help. But the pain only got worse.

By the time we got to the house and took the groceries inside, I could not stand up straight. I was nauseous and in even more pain. I went back to mom's house, missing my appointment to view the apartment. My mom made me a hot cup of tea. I went from the couch to the floor praying and asking God what was going on? The Holy Spirit told me it was my appendix. Prior to this, I had undergone so many surgeries, I refused to have another one. I laid there in so much pain. As I continued to drink tea, I began to vomit and my temperature rose to 104 degrees.

My mom was constantly repeating, you need to go to the hospital. I was talking out of my head and not making any sense. Mom insisted that I go to the hospital, but I continued laying on the floor sweating and moaning and whimpering. She told me to look at my kids, who were huddling together crying. I assured them that I was okay. I just did not want another surgery. I constantly cried out to God to help me. I believed my mom was praying along with my little ones who at this time were two and four. I continued crying out to God.

The doorbell rang. Mom opened the door. It was my cousin. I was very surprised to see her because she didn't visit often, and without calling first. She came in carrying a long white plastic bag tied at the bottom.

I asked, "Is everyone okay?"

"Yes" She responded. "I came to bring this to you."

As she passed that bag to me, I asked, "What is this?"

"Your Christmas gift from your godson."

"It's not Christmas. He knows Christmas is next month," I responded.

My cousin said, "Yes, he knows but he insisted I bring it now."

I untied the knot – it was a long coat!

"Yes, he insisted that I bring it to you today. He wants you to take it now. I guess he was excited. He insisted that I bring it before he came home from school."

While standing there seemingly confused, she asked, "What's wrong?" I was beginning to vomit into a bucket. Then she noticed how wet I was from sweating and now vomiting. My clothes were wet, and I went into a fetal position. In a panicked way she asked again, "What's wrong?"

My mom responded, "Take her to the hospital."

I did not reveal what the Holy Spirit revealed to me. I continued to lay there until I saw the fear on the faces of my babies. I tried to stand. She took the plastic off my coat and

GOD! IF YOU ARE REAL, SHOW ME!

helped me put it on. I kissed my babies and mom. My cousin and mom helped me to the car.

When we got to the Emergency Room, she went in for a wheelchair. I continued vomiting in the bucket I took from the house. Once inside, they took me to the radiation area for an ultrasound. The technician started the procedure by inserting a tube into my stomach through my nose! Then they took me to have the ultrasound. When he put the paddle on my stomach, puss began to come through the tube. I was in so much pain. He made a call and then I was rushed out and into emergency surgery. My appendix had ruptured. Then I realized that I could have died as that poison filled my body. After surgery I began thanking God for sparing my life. As I thought of my kids, these scriptures came to me –

Isaiah 55:8-9:

> *For my thoughts are not your thoughts, neither are your ways my ways, saith the Lord. For as the heavens are higher than the earth, so are my ways higher than your ways, and my thoughts than your thoughts. (KJV)*

Psalms 103:11:

> *For as the heaven is high above the earth, so great is his mercy toward them that fear him. (KJV)*

I thanked God for His mercy towards me. I trusted God for sparing my life, yet ignorant and stubborn of His word and lacking wisdom. The Holy Spirit had informed me that my appendix was inflamed, but all I could think of was what I wanted, not considering that God was even involved in this.

Now, I'm thinking that I can't move for a while. I'm stuck. But my mom was happy for us to be there. But after the last time we left, the room we slept in was turned into a den. So, with my mom working nights, I put the kids in her bed, and I slept on the floor. The kids slept wild, and I was afraid of getting kicked while sleeping with them. I didn't want any problems if they kicked in my incision. So, I made a pallet on the flood by the bed.

A few weeks before all this took place, I had gone to a warehouse in South Holland called "The Bible League." They not only send new Bibles around the world, but they are open to the public. What an awesome ministry, I thought. It was also a day center for the elderly. They sat at a long table repairing damaged Bibles that were offered free to the public. Anyone could take no more than two Bibles. There was also a table with all types of Christian books and cassettes of the Bible and sermons. There were also children's Bibles and Bible stories. On that table, you could take as many books as you liked.

The last time I was there, before the surgery, I literally found a diamond in the rough. It was a book about Smith Wigglesworth. I read that Smith Wigglesworth read nothing but the Bible – no newspapers or other books. From that info I really felt he didn't write a book. But this was a book about his faith. I remembered how excited I was to get my hands on this book.

As I laid on the floor recovering from surgery and the kids were in school, I laid there talking to God in my discouragement. I'm so grateful to God for sparing my life. Also, I could get in bed while the kids were in school. But I felt another stumbling block, another interruption for a stable home and life for my children. While I laid there with running tears, I could hear the Lord say, "I got your kids and they are OK," because they were His; He lent them to me to teach them His ways.

Hearing these encouraging words from the Lord, tears flooded my eyes while I felt I lost with very little fight left within me. Then, Smith Wigglesworth's book on faith came to mind. I got up to get the book and began reading.

Now prior to this, my pastor, Evangelist Jones died. She was an amazing woman of God and awesome prophetess. She'd look at you as if she could see your soul. Her ministry shaped my faith. I don't know if it was how she'd say, "Oooh, look at God!" that I allowed God to stretch my faith. But I wanted to brag on God every day by testifying to her and others about what God had done for me.

At the end of Bible study on a Wednesday night in her home basement, we formed a circle to pray out. After prayer, she got the oil and laid hands on each of us. She'd simply say, "Receive ye the Holy Ghost." I felt my body quiver as she prayed for others. I was praying with her while saying, "Do it, Jesus!" When she laid hands on me, saying, "Receive ye the Holy Ghost", I collapsed to the floor speaking in an unknown tongue, as my pastor interpreted my praise to God.

My mom and aunt came and worshipped with us at Evangelist Jones' church on the corner of 75th and Rhodes. After her death, my cousin and I went to other churches looking for another Evangelist Jones. At a prayer meeting, I met a lady telling me about her church. She told me of a Bishop Reed. I told my mom about his church which was not too far from mom's house, on 115th and State Street. My mom and her sister started going every week. They liked it so they both joined. They said that though he sits as he preaches, but he's a good pastor and a great teacher.

I had not visited there before. I heard that since there were many of their generation, it would be good for them. So, I continued visiting other churches. I said I was looking for one with lots of kids for my children's sake. But when it left my lips, I knew deep down I was still looking for another Evangelist Jones.

I was just finishing up my book, laying there praising God. It was Sunday. I got up to get the kids ready for church. My mom was taking them with her. As I laid there thanking God for His protection and healing, I could hear in my spirit to get up and go to the church where my mom and aunt had gone. I asked God. How? My mom was already gone. I had no way of getting there.

In my spirit I heard, "Get up and get dressed. Go to the house across the street and ask John if you can buy one of his cars."

John and his brother, Harry, bought junk cars, fixed them up to sell them. They drove some themselves. Many were parked on the street. I saw one that caught my eye. A bright yellow car with a black racing stripe along both sides. At this time, I didn't have one dollar, but I was pumped full of faith. I asked him how much he wanted for the car.

He responded, "$300."

Wow I thought, there's that $300 again.

I teared up remembering how Evangelist Jones prayed a $3.00 to $300 blessing over me before she died. This blessing continues to live on.

I asked, "Is that $300 down?"

He said, "No." He gave me the keys from his pocket.

I asked, "Can I pay you as I get it?" I assured him that I would pay him.

I had my purse and cane, so I went right to the car. I cried all the way to the church, praising God. After the surgery, I was very weak on my right side. I don't know if the weakness was due to the rupture or the surgery itself, so I used a cane. I did find driving to be a bit of a challenge, but I took my time.

When I got there, the service had started. There were many cars parked on the street. I was praying I could find a close parking. When I got to the corner in front of the church, I could hear the singing of the choir. I got nervous as I sat there, worrying about walking in late with all eyes on me. I almost talked myself out of going in. Then, conviction came upon me. How God made a mighty way for me to get here, and all the provisions he provided. I had to push past the fears. Being here for the first time, I didn't know where to sit, or if there would be any seats left. Well, I made it up the stairs and walked in, opening one of the double glass doors. Just as I thought, all eyes were on me. I looked around for mom and the kids. I saw my son waving for me to come sit by them. I thanked God that there was room for me.

The pastor had just started his sermon. The Overseer Reed stopped his words. Before I could take my seat, the pastor spoke to me saying, "I know who you are and if I didn't see you today, I was coming to you. Your mom told me you were home from the hospital."

I continued to my seat as he spoke. When I sat down, he continued his sermon, as some continued to look at me puzzled. I was so focused on trying to find another Evangelist Jones, that I could barely hear God say, 'You are home'.

I heard the overseer was sick and preached from a chair in the pulpit. Thoughts were scrambling in my mind. "I can't go through this again. I can't lose another pastor." Then I heard in my spirit, "She took me as far as she could." At the end of the service, he prayed for me. As we prepared to leave, my mom expressed how surprised she was to see me. I explained what happened and she was shocked to see that beautiful car – clean, no dents and shining bright.

I drove home and parked in front of mom's house. I decided to go to the store. Being out for the first time felt good. I turned the key. Nothing happened. It would not start. I checked the oil. It was full and so was the gas, according to the readings. I went to get the neighbor who sold me the car.

He came right out, "What's wrong?"

"It won't start," I responded.

After checking under the hood, he asked, "Did it stop on you, or drive sluggish?"

"No, it drove like a new car. What's wrong? Why did you ask that?"

He responded, "The transmission was blown. It needs a new one."

I thought to myself, 'I can't get that fixed and pay for the car.'

He closed the hood and asked me for the keys. "I didn't realize it was in that bad shape. I would not have sold you that car," he said.

I went into the house rejoicing, knowing that car was actually a blessing. It fulfilled its purpose to get me to that church at that day and time; and he didn't expect me to pay for that car and fix it myself.

"Thank you, Jesus" I spoke aloud.

I remained at that church about fifteen years or so. Overseer Reed was an amazing man of God – full of faith and abundant love for God. I learned much from him along my faith journey. When he passed, I was saddened that I hadn't known him longer, but I was not broken. Thinking back to what God had said about Evangelist Jones, Overseer Reed also took me as far as he was supposed to.

One Way

Romans 2:19-21:

> *And art confident that thou thyself art a guide of the blind, a light of them which are in darkness, An instructor of the foolish, a teacher of babes, which hast the form of knowledge and of the truth in the law. Thou therefore which teachest another, teachest thou not thyself? thou that preachest a man should not steal, dost thou steal? (KJV)*

It was early evening. I had just dropped off a friend at home. Coming out of a one-way street, I noticed a sign when I looked into my rear-view mirror -- a very large sign. Huge, I might add, which read 'DO NOT ENTER'. I thought to myself, "I've never seen that sign before." I stopped at the stop sign at the top of the hill and turned around and looked back at the sign. It was not that big -- in fact it was normal size. I returned to the rear-view mirror and was totally amazed that it was huge! I went from window to mirror, and the views were totally different.

At this point, I was very puzzled. I could hear God saying, "Do you know what would happen if you would turn to drive back the way you came, driving towards the sign? It could be dangerous." Anyone walking or driving towards the sign knows they'll see the traffic coming towards them, and move out the way. In that area, many walk in the street because of the damaged sidewalks. Also, many could unexpectedly cross right in front of you with no reason to look behind them, since it is a one-way street.

Signs are there for everyone's protection. Then it came to me that this is starting to look like a lesson from the Lord. I asked God, "What are you telling me?" I was in complete denial. God had spoken to me already, but I wasn't going to help Him out. At this time, I was struggling. I've been divorced for a little over a year. My pastor died recently. I visited many churches. There was no one to take over her ministry. She taught strict holiness. I was saved and Holy Ghost-filled. We were taught that we are the light – an example for others. Through trial after trial, God always brought me out victorious. God used me to lead many souls to Christ -- those that watched my life and some who came to church with me and my children.

I was a single mother with two small children. When I cried out to God for the welfare of my children to be fed and clothed, also to keep a roof over our heads, God never failed and showed up every time.

Then secretly, for me the 'Old Man' started appearing in my flesh. It may have been a secret to others, but God saw it before I knew it. This scripture came to me –

Romans 7:18-20:

> *For I know that in me (that is, in my flesh,) dwelleth no good thing: for to will is present with me; but how to perform that which is good I find not. For the good that I would I do not: but the evil which I would not, that I do. Now if I do that I would not, it is no more I that do it, but sin that dwelleth in me. (KJV)*

Then, concerning that 'Old Man', my sinful nature, God spoke His words to me –

Ephesians 4:21-24:

> *if indeed you have heard Him and have been taught in Him, just as truth is in Jesus, that, in reference to your former way of life, you are to rid yourselves of the old self, which is being corrupted in accordance with the lusts of deceit, and that you are to be renewed in the spirit of your minds, and to put on the new self, which in the likeness of God has been created in righteousness and holiness of the truth. (NASB)*

While I was wrestling in my flesh, the word of God flooded my very soul. But I allowed myself to push past God's spirit of escape.

I Corinthians 10:13:

> *No temptation has overtaken you except something common to mankind; and God is faithful, so He will not allow you to be tempted beyond what you are able, but with the temptation will provide the way of escape also, so that you will be able to endure it. (NASB)*

According to God's word, He promises a way of escape when temptation is planted in our mind. But it really starts in conversation.

II Timothy 2:16:

> *But avoid worldly and empty chatter, for it will lead to further ungodliness. (NASB)*

Then, it's activated in our heart and continues to allow our flesh to grow. Temptation gets stronger as God's word grows weaker and harder to hear. God presents His word as to convict our hearts. But God does not make us do anything. He gives us free will to make our own decisions, whether good or bad. We are well aware of the wrong decision that lingers in your mind, yet we allow the temptation to remain. We think of it often and halt between two opinions. Now we find ourselves looking for loopholes or even the fine print in the word of God, because the flesh wants to give in to the temptation.

Even though I Corinthians 10:13 says that we are not tempted above which we are able to bear, and God will provide a way of escape, I'm now saying to God, "this is way above my being able to bear." I made excuses for my actions. My mind shifted to find a scripture that I could stand on that could excuse my actions.

I found I John 1:19:

If we confess our sins, He is faithful and righteous, so that He will forgive us our sins and cleanse us from all unrighteousness. (NASB)

After reading this scripture, I then allowed this to be my excuse to follow through with the sin that entered my heart. At this point, I had completely talked myself into it -- just walked into the enemy's camp without the guidance of the Holy Spirit, as if I muzzled the Spirit of God.

As I followed the crying out of my flesh, I thought about what I called 'the fine print'. God will forgive me for unrighteousness. Then before I made it to my destination, my soul cried out yet again in warning, saying, "What would separate you from the love of God?" In the past, I always said I would never sin against God for a few minutes of pleasure. But here I am giving in to lustful pleasures. Then, afterwards, I started beating myself up because it wasn't worth it. All I could think of was how God felt. I felt like one of them who yelled out, "Crucify Him!" I also thought about how I could do this after three years of celibacy. There's no enjoyment when you think of how you hurt God by your disobedience. I repented immediately, but my prayer seemed to have stayed in the room. I didn't feel God's presence – just a quiet emptiness. God does forgive but I didn't think about forgiving myself.

My mind went to Hosea 1:2:

The beginning of the word of the Lord by Hosea. And the Lord said to Hosea, Go, take unto thee a wife of whoredoms and children of whoredoms: for the land hath committed great whoredom, departing from the Lord. (KJV)

I knew exactly what God was saying to me. God is our husbandman. When we step out of His will by whoring after things not of His will, we allow sin to enter in impregnating us with the ways of the world.

St. John 17:15:

> *I pray not that thou shouldest take them out of the world, but that thou shouldest keep them from the evil. (KJV)*

That 'One Way' sign spoke so much in my life. I know I wanted to be an example and not a stumbling block.

Romans 14:13:

> *Let us not therefore judge one another any more: but judge this rather, that no man put a stumblingblock or an occasion to fall in his brother's way. (KJV)*

Many are definitely watching me, but most of all, my children are watching me. They were taught to not only do what I say, but also do what I do. I felt this wouldn't be a difficult task to live openly as I followed God. I love God. He's been so good to me and my little family. I've seen this before – when everything is going well you may not hear anything from those that live not for God. But when you fall or step one foot outside of your faith, then comes the criticism. They say, "Aren't you saved?" Some would go further saying, "I knew it wasn't nothing to this 'saved' stuff. Y'all are all hypocrites!" I knew my actions reflected on God. In turn, my actions would push them further from the cross and all it stood for.

At this point I was more concerned about them that watch my life as I reflected God's image. I was so angry with myself thinking I don't want to fall again. The opportunity presented itself again. This time I fasted to kill that lustful flesh.

As representatives of Christ, our mission is to represent God in both word and deed. We are His living epistles – God's ambassadors. We are as a living Bible, revealing God's nature – His love, His grace, forgiveness, His glory, mirroring His image and declaring His truth. This life that we answered the call to live is doable and livable when we live a life centered in prayer and close communication with God, including studying His word. This is the only way we should continue to go if we want a close relationship with God. We are His friend, and friends don't do anything to jeopardize friendship.

The 'ONE WAY DO NOT ENTER' sign is a regulatory traffic sign. Drivers encountering this sign must travel in the direction that the arrow is pointing. Travelers must not travel in the opposite direction of the sign due to the risk of a head-on collision. As believers, we go the wrong way when we follow unbelievers. Unbelievers can be a stumbling block to God's signs.

St. Mark 16:17-18:

> *And these signs shall follow them that believe; In my name shall they cast out devils; they shall speak with new tongues; They shall take up serpents; and if they drink any deadly thing, it shall not hurt them; they shall lay hands on the sick, and they shall recover. (KJV)*

Romans 12:1-2:

> *Therefore I urge you, brothers and sisters, by the mercies of God, to present your bodies as a living and holy sacrifice, acceptable to God, which is your spiritual service of worship. And do not be conformed to this world, but be transformed by the renewing of your mind, so that you may prove what the will of God is, that which is good and acceptable and perfect. (NASB)*

Lessons in the Storm

JOB 37:5-7 & 13-14

God thunders wondrously with His voice,
Doing great things which we do not comprehend.
For to the snow He says, 'Fall on the earth,'
And to the downpour and the rain, 'Be strong.'
He seals the hand of every person,
So that all people may know His work.
Whether for correction, or for His earth,
Or for goodness, He causes it to happen.
"Listen to this, Job;
Stand and consider the wonders of God. (NASB)

I've experienced a great rain of God's strength traveling in the car with my young daughter and two friends heading to the mall. I was traveling on I-57 South. All our windows were open – enjoying the sunshine and the cool breeze. Then I noticed an unusual darkness ahead on the road that seemed to stretch across both north and south expressways. It seemed to be from the sky to the ground. The traffic began to slow down. As we drew closer, the sky gradually started darkening, then a light rain. While continuing toward the darkness, the wind began blowing. We had to close the windows due to the blowing in of the rain. The closer we got to the darkness, the more intense the rain. The traffic went from sixty to thirty, then five mph – barely moving. Some cars started merging to park on the shoulder. The rain and darkness were very dense. There were no headlights ahead – only dull taillights. The hard downpour of rain never seemed to let up.

Looking through the rearview mirror, it was total darkness and dull headlights behind. The cars were bumper-to-bumper. I'd never seen such a storm as this. It was so frightening watching other pull over on the shoulder, and I wanted to pull over as well. I could barely see the cars around me. We were all praying silently. All we could hear was the hard downpour and the loud swishing of the windshield wipers. There was no light of hope ahead. The sudden darkness was as if we were driving through a long tunnel with no end. I was slowly proceeding forward. Then the car in front of me also pulled over to the shoulder. Then I had an open path to continue going forth. It seemed to get darker. We continued praying silently.

While driving, I nervously sat on the edge of my seat, paying close attention not to hit anyone and trying to keep from being hit. We prayed for the storm to pass over us. No sooner praying this for the sixth time, and before I could add 'in Jesus' name, Amen', just as suddenly as we went into the dense darkness, it was bright and sunny – no rain. I thought it had just stopped, but when I looked through the rearview mirror, I was absolutely stunned. I couldn't believe what I saw, so I pulled over onto the shoulder, parked and got out of the car. I discovered that the rain didn't stop – we drove out of the storm. We all stepped out of the car in complete disbelief, or did our eyes deceive us? We stood there gazing at this great mysterious storm!! As we faced the highway from which we came, we were standing in dry sunshine, looking back at the dark storm as it continued.

It was hard to believe that I actually drove right out of a violent storm. I looked from one side to the other. Now I saw the cars that were in front of me that gave up and were now parking on the shoulder just feet from coming out of the storm. Slowly, other cars trickled out, as well. Also, on the expressway heading north, the traffic had come to a complete halt. It was a parking lot for blocks going into the darkness.

That entire experience was seared into my mind. We stood there for over twenty minutes. When others pulled over, getting out of their cars, as well, we all gazed at this strange occurrence.

As we proceeded on our way, I could hear the voice of the Lord speaking to me about our troubles as His children. He showed me how we are never alone. In Daniel 3:24-37, the three Hebrew boys were bound and thrown into a fiery furnace. But when they looked into the furnace, there were four men walking around and the fourth one was like the form of the Son of God. The fire did not singe their hair or clothing, nor was the smell of smoke on them, as if there was no power in the fire.

I relate our troubles to a boisterous storm and feel God's presence in our great times of storms, and our dark troubles. We learn many lessons if we listen to God's voice. He will speak during our storms. Looking back to how I went in – there was no way around it. I had to go through it. I went in and I drove out – not immediately, but I came out. If there was an entrance, there was definitely an exit.

Thinking about how panicked I was, and all the turmoil around me, I never thought of pulling over onto the shoulder until I saw others doing so. I was praying, but I seemed to be more influenced by those around me. Suddenly, I started thinking, am I doing the right thing by second guessing what was within my spirit? I thought, maybe they know something that I don't.

But Proverbs 3:5-6 says:

> *Trust in the Lord with all thine heart; and lean not unto thine own understanding.*
>
> *In all thy ways acknowledge him, and he shall direct thy paths. (KJV)*

We are not to be led by those around us but be led by God. Ask God what to do and not allowing panic to enter in causing fear to take the lead. I know fear and faith don't travel the same path.

II Timothy 1:7:

For God hath not given us the spirit of fear; but of power , and of love, and of a sound mind. (KJV)

What I took from that whole experience was that our trials – as dark as they may seem – make us feel so all alone. But you're not! God is right there. Also, we should stop to learn the lessons in our troubles. I later realized that God could show us better than tell us. Just as many parables in the Bible, we are not likely to forget a demonstration.

I remembered that God told me, "Don't stop. Keep moving." How many times will fear gripped us, that we stopped or took a detour in an attempt to bypass trouble, only for it to come back another way another time? It's always best to embrace the challenge by praying and studying God's word. When God blessed us to come out unharmed, I turned around and saw all the people that stopped only feet from coming out of the storm, I really wanted to run in yelling, "Come just a little further. Come out! Keep moving. It's not that far. Come out."

But as always, I'm now on the outside looking in. But while I was in the storm, I saw the darkness of a fierce storm. The fear of no way out gripped my faith. Most importantly, the best lesson learned, as a believer, is no matter how hard it seems, of how dark it becomes, never stop in the midst of a storm or seek a detour. But when you settle down, don't ask, "What have I done, God?" Instead ask God, "What is it, God, that you want me to learn from this?"

That storm taught me so much about myself. My first human instinct was fear; even with all I knew about God and His love for me. Then to question God? It did not even cross my mind that I'm so important to God that He allowed this encounter just for me to just get it! Then again, why not – He sees our struggles.

Jeremiah 29:11:

'For I know the plans that I have for you,' declares the Lord, 'plans for prosperity and not for disaster, to give you a future and a hope.' (NASB)

According to God's word, it's all in His plan for His children.

I've gone through trials when I knew -- this is it. I can't do it. It's too hard. I think that I've disappointed God far too many times and he's tired. "Why, God," I'd ask. "Why can't I just get it?" Only later I come to realize that His plans for me far exceed my own fears. I realize that the twenty-to-thirty-minute encounter in that storm was real. It was frightening, as well as eye-opening. I thought I was confident in my relationship with God. I thought that I trusted in Him without wavering. But there are times and trials set up just to show you who you are as well as what's on the inside of you. This way we'll know where we fall short and also where we need to come up.

Thank you, God. My eternity is with you. You are the author and finisher of my faith.

Lamentation Part 1: The Passionate Expression of Grief or Sorrow

When you lose someone close to your heart, it's painful. But when you lose two, possibly three, it's absolutely devastating – especially, when it all happens in a week!

St. John 14:1-4:

> *Let not your heart be troubled: ye believe in God, believe also in me. In my Father's house are many mansions: if it were not so, I would have told you. I go to prepare a place for you. And if I go and prepare a place for you, I will come again, and receive you unto myself; that where I am, there ye may be also. And whither I go ye know, and the way ye know. (KJV)*

Amos 4:12b:

> *... prepare to meet thy God (KJV)*

It was months before my son died that I found myself preparing him, with a sense of urgency, to be ready to meet the Lord. At that time, I didn't realize that was what I was doing. I felt it was just in case he was ever in trouble. I clearly wasn't anticipating anything. I often told both children that whenever they needed God, to call on His holy name. I also taught them to stay repentant.

I would find myself in the middle of the night, getting in his bed to hold him. I talked to him, asking him. "Do you really believe or is it just because I told you to believe?"

He'd mumble, "I believe."

Then, I'd ask him, "Did you pray, tonight?"

He'd respond with a nod, "Yes, I did."

Again, I'd ask, "Did you repent?"

He'd respond, being frustrated, "Yes, momma, always."

"One more thing, and I'll let you get back to sleep…"

He'd respond with, "Hmmm?"

"If you were ever in any kind of trouble, what would you do? Who would you call?"

He didn't respond, so I asked again. "If you were in trouble, Tyree, who would you call?"

"Jesus, momma, I'd call Jesus."

I responded, "Yes, that's right, son. He's everywhere. Always know that I may not be able to hear you, but God will always hear His children when they call."

He responded, half asleep, "I know, momma. You told me. Why you keep telling me that?"

"I really need you to know and understand that." I responded.

I would lay there for a while, holding and kissing his frowned face. Then, I'd return to my bed, praying and telling God not to allow my kids and family to leave this earth unless they can see your face in peace.

I didn't understand the sudden urgency. And why wasn't I doing the same with my daughter? I remember when I came to the Lord, God told me that these were His children. He loaned them to me to teach them His ways and to love Him. I took these words very seriously and did so to the best of my abilities. I didn't fully understand, due to the fact that I hadn't known God that long myself. I learned of God's true existence in my mid-20's.

I'd watch TV with them explaining what part God played in the show. That was any show – even cartoons. If evil won in the end, they were not permitted to watch the show again. The only cartoons they were allowed to watch were Christian cartoons on the Gospel Network. They were definitely not permitted to watch movies with evil intent.

When I came into holiness, we were taught to fast three days and nights, twice a month. I also had them to fast two days a week, twice a month, from morning till noon. They ate lunch and dinner. Many times, I was accused of being too zealous. But to me, I was just doing my job as God said and as their mother.

We always sat at the table together as a family for meals. That time was used to hear of their day. I would use their stories to teach them about God. Prior to his passing, many times I would choke on my food as I was talking, focusing more on my son. Strangely, it seemed as though I was preparing him for a trip away from home, away from me. We rehearsed it so he wouldn't forget anything I taught him.

I started noticing that I didn't seem to do the same for his sister, as if she wasn't leaving. Yet they were both the same. But the intensity of the outpouring of information seemed to be for him. As though he was going far away, being on his own and out of my reach. Later, this scripture came to me when I remembered these times and what I did.

Deuteronomy 11:19-20:

> *And ye shall teach them your children, speaking of them when thou sittest in thine house, and when thou walkest by the way, when thou liest down, and when thou risest up. And thou shalt write them upon the door posts of thine house, and upon thy gates (KJV)*

As God gave me scriptures, I'd post them on the medicine cabinet in the bathroom and also in the kitchen on the refrigerator door. They were there for them, as well as for me, to read and learn. It was encouragement because we all went through so much.

Proverbs 3:5-6:

> *Trust in the Lord with all thine heart; and lean not unto thine own understanding. In all thy ways acknowledge him, and he shall direct thy paths. (KJV)*

Ephesians 3:20:

> *Now unto him that is able to do exceeding abundantly above all that we ask or think, according to the power that worketh in us. (KJV)*

They also knew Psalms 23:

The Lord is my shepherd; I shall not want. He maketh me to lie down in green pastures: he leadeth me beside the still waters. He restoreth my soul: he leadeth me in the paths of righteousness for his name's sake. Yea, though I walk through the valley of the shadow of death, I will fear no evil: for thou art with me; thy rod and thy staff they comfort me. Thou preparest a table before me in the presence of mine enemies: thou anointest my head with oil; my cup runneth over. Surely goodness and mercy shall follow me all the days of my life: and I will dwell in the house of the Lord for ever. (KJV)

Another thing I often taught them was about being obedient. I'd tell them how God honors obedience, even to me. I'd tell them, if I told them to play or stay in the backyard, within the perimeter I set within the fenced yard, God would honor it and protect them no matter what was going on – be it shootings, kidnappings, etc., it would not touch them. God would keep them safe. I stood heavily on obedience to the point that I would tell them if they lied before the end of the day, they would bump their head. They believed it because it, generally, would happen.

Well, thinking about this today, I may have gone a little overboard. This clearly was manipulation. But now, thinking back, all I could think of is that I wanted them to be honest and obedient at all costs.

It was early Monday morning, on the day my son died, which was five days after his 18th birthday. He came to help me take my dad to dialysis. Both of my dad's legs were amputated and my son was the only one who had the strength to carry him. Even with dad's water weight, he could carry him to the car. My brothers all struggled doing so.

The Sunday night before, my son asked if he could help a neighbor move. He also wanted to know if I would be able to get someone to help me put my dad in the car and back in the house when we returned. My son came with me often without a mumbling word. So, for him to ask if he could help someone else, and if I could then be able to find someone to help me, this allowed me to find help and give him that break. I was not able to get anyone to put dad in the car, so my son came with me to do so. I was not able to drop him at his friend's house, so he asked to be dropped off on the side of the road, a block from McDonald's. He would meet up with his sister to eat and then take the bus to the neighbor's house.

Thinking back, we rushed to get to the drop-off location. He jumped out of the car, and I didn't get a chance to kiss him as I always did with both children. I watched him as I prayed that he didn't get hit by a car as he walked on the side with the flow of traffic. I felt harm coming upon him, so I yelled for him to walk on the other side of the street so he would be seen by oncoming traffic. I moved on knowing that he'd be okay with all the blessed oil that was on his prayed over hat and shoes.

After my dad's appointment, my brother met me at dad's house to assist me with him. I came in, set up my dad's dinner and then went out to set his garbage on the curb for Tuesday pick up.

During that time, very few people had cell phones. I called my son at the neighbor's home phone, where the kids hung out, to see if he was done helping the neighbor move.

He informed me, "The guy we were supposed to help, never showed up."

I asked, "Where is your sister?"

"We're both sitting on the porch with our friends."

"Well, stay on the block because I'm on my way to pick you up to take you home."

He replied, "Okay."

Fifteen minutes later, as I was getting in my car, my brother ran to me saying, "Your son had been shot, and they don't think he'll make it!" My God, I thought! My brother offered to drive me to Christ Hospital, as I began to shake uncontrollably. At the time, I was in Dolton during rush hour traffic – 3:30 to 4:00 pm. I told him, "Thanks, but I'll drive. I need to talk to God." My brother claimed to be an unbeliever and I didn't want any hindrances. I knew he loved my son, but at that time it had to be just me and God. I really can't remember how I got there so fast, or what street I took, as I was praying.

When I got there, my daughter ran to me crying. I held her as she cried. As I attempted to hold back tears, I asked to see my son. He laid there so still with his head bandaged and covered with a sheet. The right side of his face was swollen and discolored darker. I began to shake again seeing him lying there lifeless. I tried to kiss his face but was not able to for all the machines and cords attached to him. Then a flash came to me of him getting out of the car without me kissing him. I cried even more when God showed me the times, I got in his bed holding and kissing him. That gave me a moment of peace. I asked myself, did he know how much I loved him?

So, I was able to kiss his hand and arm. He was shot in the head and in the knee. I asked the nurses, "Why isn't he in surgery to remove the bullets?" I was told that when he was shot in the head, he lost the majority of his brain mass. I was shown an x-ray that showed a lot of white spots which I was told were skull fragments in the remainder of his brain. The other parts of his brain were in his hat which was also on the ground at the site of the shooting.

I pushed past all that was told to me. I believed God for a miracle – I knew He was able. I began micro-remembering all I was taught about God's abilities – faith without doubt. All the testimonies I'd heard over the years – God can create another brain. He will be okay.

I began to kiss his hand harder and pressing it even harder to my face and lips. I was constantly telling him how much I loved him and that he needed to fight! When a nurse came to me asking if he was an organ donor, I ignored her. I told her that I wanted him to have every chance possible.

Again, they showed me the x-ray of his skull filled with white specks. She was saying that he was brain-dead, but I knew he was still there. The nurse said that he was brain-dead and not coming back from there. I didn't want to leave his side. I knew my daughter was in good hands with praying people and I didn't want my son to be alone. I felt he was afraid although he never regained consciousness. They told me the machine was breathing for him. Again, I was asked if he was a donor.

Then, I remembered that when he got his license, he chose to be an organ donor. I had him to have that choice removed. I thought that if he was in a minor accident, they might just harvest his body parts – not just his organs. I assured him I would let this information be known. I never thought in a million years, I'd have to be the one making that decision.

Next, two ladies approached me to sign papers to harvest his organs. I told them I wasn't ready – I wanted to continue sitting with him. I was told that I could continue to sit with him, so I signed the papers to donate his organs. Then, they began to pick him apart, in my mind, asking if I would also donate his eyes and arms. They said no one would know what was missing.

I couldn't take it any longer! I refused, telling them, "Organs only!"

At that time, making these decisions alone was so difficult. I went back to be with him after checking on my daughter to see if she wanted to see him again. She did. When she saw him, she cried falling to the floor. I hugged her, praying for her peace. Her friends came to take her to the chapel.

Later, I was told my dad could've possibly received my son's kidneys. No one considered at the time whether they were a match. It was mentioned the following week.

I remember how both women ran out of the room so quickly, after I signed. I felt like they stole my son from me.

I pray that ROBI (Regional Organ Bank of Illinois) has gotten more caring after people sign over loved ones to them. I felt that one of them should have stayed with me, at least until he was taken to surgery. Later, I went to the ROBI office downtown to apply for an open position as a grief counselor; I was told they had no need.

It bothered me so bad that I could not hold him again, that I grabbed the first pieces of paper I saw – a blank envelope and an ink pen. I began to sketch an image of me sitting on the curb where he was shot, crying out to God with my daughter crying and holding onto me. Drawing this seemed to give me a bit of comfort. I'd look at it daily until thoughts came to mind of how he died in the streets like a thug. This was not the way he was. He died by the very thing that I did not allow in my home – no guns, not even a water gun. So how God? Why?

I've forgotten about the poem I wrote on the other side of the envelope where I drew the picture. I'd forgotten until now. When I started writing this book, I saw it.

TO HOLD YOU, SAY GOODBYE
ALL THE WHILE, ASKING WHY?
ALWAYS BEEN THE THREE OF US
THREE FOR AS FAR BACK
AS I COULD SEE.
NOW SEPARATED
FOR THE FIRST TIME
YOU PROMISED
AND SHE (FROM ME).
HOW COULD THIS BE
DEATH DIVIDE WHEN GUIDED
BY THE HAND OF MAN
BUT MORE BLESSED
WHEN THE HOURGLASS
RUNS OUT OF SAND.
CAN ONE'S LIFE
FIND THE WAY BACK
TO THE CLOSENESS
ONCE WAS
NOOO LACK.

As I wrote this poem, 2 Samuel 22:2 came to me:

The Lord is my rock and my fortress and my deliverer. (NASB)

Lamentation Part 2: Urgency to Repent

My mom was in the same hospital at the same time, recovering from a stroke. She was to be released that week from rehab. All my siblings agreed she couldn't handle the news of what was going on with her grandson, in her current medical state. But the more I thought about it, knowing my mom, I knew she would have been furious with us if we made any decision for her or without her input.

My brother and I went to talk to her doctor. We explained to him that her grandson was down in the emergency room. They would soon be taking him to surgery to harvest his organs. I knew she would have wanted to see him because they were very close. The doctor agreed and in doing so, he instructed the nurse to give her a sedative. He also insisted that she remain in the wheelchair. She was not to stand.

When she came into the ER, I told my brother to take her on his left side where from her height and position he just looked asleep. All the trauma was on the other side; the whole right side was dark and very swollen. Mom stayed and held his other hand where the IV was. She teared up a little while talking to him.

After 30 minutes, she was calm and returned to her room. Many family members and siblings went with her.

I just couldn't leave him alone. I felt he was still there. I began to get so nauseated that I really had to vomit. Knowing I couldn't make it to the bathroom, a nurse grabbed 2 large bath towels from a nearby cart. She put it to my mouth just in time because I could not hold it. Afterwards, I looked at him, and I knew he was gone. A vivid picture came to my mind -- when he came into the world, I vomited the same way at that time. They put a pan to my mouth. My heart was crushed, but I knew he was gone. That was my confirmation from God that it was so. Again, I said, "See you later," and kissed his hand and foot. I professed to him, "I'll always love you." I was able to leave out one door, while watching them roll him away to surgery out the other door.

I couldn't go see my mom. I knew she would pick up on my broken heart. I wanted her home. I didn't want my presence to hinder that. I knew she would feel my pain, and I didn't realize that she was hurting for me, as well. The truth was that I needed her so much. I wanted to lay my head in her lap and cry. I knew that would only hurt her more.

So, I went home – my cousin drove me home in my car. I went to mom's house to find my daughter. When I found her, she was drunk and crying. Her friends felt the need to numb her pain with lots of alcohol. I took her to my mom's house where she collapsed on the sidewalk by the stairs.

She laid there crying, saying, "I'm not going in until my brother comes home." About an hour later, I was able to get her in the house. I managed to get her into a hot bath which always comforted and calmed her. She cried the entire time, yelling, "I want to go with my brother. What happened? I thought God was supposed to protect us. Why! He didn't help my brother. Why! Missed everybody in that crowd but my brother. We were always in church praying. You made us fast and pray, for what? Why!"

I really didn't have an answer for her. I had my own unanswered questions. So, I allowed her to rant and get it out.

I didn't understand. My thoughts went to how I tried to do everything right. Yes, I messed up sometimes, but not on purpose. I did as God asked of me – to raise them to love Him. I repented nightly even more so during the times I messed up. Then, I thought about the time I had the abortion. Was this my punishment? We didn't have much money. All I had was my babies – I always wanted to be a mother. We struggled, yes, but my babies never missed a meal. I always managed to keep a roof over our heads. I kept them in prayer, church, revivals, Bible study in church, as well as home. My son sang in the choir. He often went along when we went out on mission work.

Again, I thought, what more could I have done, God? There were times when I felt they were getting a bit ungrateful. I would take them on what I called "Gratitude Rides." I took them to shelters to read and play with the kids so the mothers could get a break. We would also drive through Lower Wacker Drive where they saw families living outside in boxes – there were no tents then. We made food plates to give to the homeless. They were also taken to impoverished neighborhoods where kids didn't have grass to play in, just dirt with broken glass, cigarette butts and garbage. I wanted them to be loving, compassionate and most of all grateful.

So, I didn't know what to tell her. I didn't understand, either. All I could say was, "God was there." I finally got her in bed. I laid there holding her as she slept. She continued whimpering and crying out in her sleep throughout the night.

The following day, I went to Leak and Sons Funeral Home to make arrangements.

It seemed as if more time had passed. He died on Monday, June 10, 1996. I held his funeral that Friday on the 14th. Everyone questioned, "What's the rush?" I didn't know, but I was led to have the funeral right away. I just wanted to get it over with. I felt an urgency to do it right away.

I made the arrangements and went to the florist to get the flowers. I had his favorite cream suit cleaned. He knew he looked good in it, and I wanted him to look good. I dropped the suit off at the funeral home. But it seemed like I just couldn't go choose his burial plot. So, my cousin, Ouida, went for me. She has recently gone on to be with the Lord.

I spoke to my mom's doctor. She wanted to come to the services. The doctor allowed her to go, but she had to be sedated.

We had four people in wheelchairs. To have the services at my present church was impossible – there were too many stairs.

I asked Pastor Trotter if I could have the funeral at his church on 103rd Street. It was a few blocks from my son's school. My son was well-liked by many. Being held on the last day of school, I knew many of the students and friends wanted to come to the service. Also, many of the school staff attended. When I made the arrangement, I asked Pastor Trotter what I owed him for the use of his facilities. He told me there was no charge and if I needed anything, to let him know. I was so grateful for his generosity. He also gave me a booklet on handling grief. Everything seemed to work out.

I couldn't understand why I couldn't get it out of my mind that he was alone and afraid. I found out later during the trial that he wasn't alone. There was an officer who stayed with him, as he laid there attempting to get up. The officer told me that he talked to him to calm him as he felt around on the ground as if he was looking for something. I was told that his hat and glasses were near, but he couldn't allow him to disturb the crime scene. The officer remembered how it affected him as he watched my son with his eyes closed, trying to get up. He said that he'd never seen anything like that before. There were pieces of his brains on his clothes and also in his hat and on the ground.

The officer also shared with me that there was an off-duty officer nearby who was working on his car when he heard the shooting. He saw two young men running towards him. Talking to a friend at the time, he had his friend call 911 to let them know that he had detained them. He had pulled his weapon insisting they stop and get on the ground. One did, the other ran between the houses, but the officer knew him from the neighborhood. He later captured him at home. Both were arrested and sentenced to thirty-two years; thirty-four years for the shooter.

My family was alerted when they were released but I really didn't want to know. I didn't want to feel what my heart wanted to feel. That was revenge, hatred and unforgiveness, my brother told me. My daughter already knew that they were released, as she was told by her cousin.

It was so unfair, I felt, that they were released after only sixteen and seventeen years for "good behavior." I thought, they are in their late thirties. They can still live a full life. I struggled with forgiveness, thinking of how their parents and family could still touch and hug them, enjoy the births of grandchildren.

One Sunday, after church, we drove down 103rd Street and passed the church where we held the funeral. My daughter recognized the guy who did the shooting. He was coming out of that church holding a baby and walking with a young lady.

That whole scene hit us like a sword in our souls. Immediately, she wanted to retaliate by running him down. I told her, "NO! He got by but he didn't get away with anything. I assured her God will deal with them.

As it is said in Romans 12:19:

> *Dearly beloved, avenge not yourselves, but rather give place unto wrath: for it is written, Vengeance is mine; I will repay, saith the Lord. (KJV)*

With much bitterness in her heart, she didn't want to hear what I was saying. I had her to pull the car over to calm down. She finally did, so when they were out of our view, in tears, she continued to proceed home.

In the beginning, I became angry as some came to me saying, "I'm sorry. I know how you feel." I'd slightly smile saying nothing. Later, after much pain in my soul, anger rose up in my heart. I started responding, "REALLY! How many of your children did you bury?"

The one lady responded, "My nephew was shot five times."

"When did he die?" I asked.

"He didn't die," was her response that caused anger in me.

"Number one – he wasn't your child. Number two – he lived." I walked off. That was way out of my character, but that was a very hard week.

After his funeral, we spent all day Saturday at the hospital visiting with my mom. She found comfort hearing my daughter sing. She heard how well she sang "Because He Lives" at an event the Saturday before his death. As she sang the song, there was a great stillness in the hall as well. This song brought peace to my mom. She also sang "Because He Lives" at her brother's funeral. That song seemed to bring her peace.

Days before his death, we went to a church service at a hall we were attending. Pastor Darlean would always ask my daughter to sing in the services. After she spoke at the Saturday service, she asked my daughter to come up to sing "Because He Lives." She sang with no emotion – just to get through the song and attempting to end the song. Pastor motioned for her to repeat from the top. The Pastor had her to continue again. On the fourth time of singing this song, she closed her eyes and poured out her heart – hand raised and eyes gushing with tears. Her brother saw her crying, and he also cried. He hated seeing her cry. As she walked off the pulpit area, there wasn't a dry eye around.

Immediately, Pastor made an urgent altar call for salvation. She went on saying, "This is an urgent call for salvation. This call is so urgent, you may leave here today, be struck by a truck and die instantly."

You could feel the presence of God. Again, Pastor belted out, "This is so serious – God is here. If you don't come, raise your hand."

Still, no one responded. She continued asking everyone to repeat the Sinner's Prayer after her. She told us to obey the Spirit of God and repeat after her. You could hear loud participation. I looked at my children. Both recited with much tears. I could see the sincerity on their faces. I held his hand, and I saw my daughter hold his other hand.

One thing I knew was that he feared God. He was still a kid, but at the end of each day, he'd repent. If we were in the car, or if someone said that some disaster was coming or if lightning came during a storm and the lights were out, he would say, "Lord, forgive me for all my sins."

Whenever we were in the car and I spotted all darkness with a clear line of light in the sky, I would tell them, "Look up. No one knows when Jesus is coming back. That thin bright ray of light could be Jesus returning."

My son would immediately close his eyes. "Speak out, Lord, forgive me for my sins."

My daughter would attempt to correct him, "Momma always says that. She's trying to scare us."

He would say it anyway. Then, I would repeat this scripture to them:

St. Mark 13:22-33:

> *But of that day and that hour knoweth no man, no, not the angels which are in heaven, neither the Son, but the Father. Take ye heed, watch and pray: for ye know not when the time is. (KJV)*

Lamentation Part 3: The Breakdown of the Family

Sunday evening, June 16, 1996, was a day I'll never forget. The Chicago Bulls won the championship. The hospital called saying that my mother was having trouble breathing. Most of the out-of-town family were leaving that night or Monday. We called family and friends; some were still at the house since my son's Homegoing.

I'll never forget how difficult it was to get to Christ Hospital. There were crowds of people celebrating in the streets blocking traffic, yelling and drinking. By the time we made it to the hospital, she had already made her transition. I heard the news before I saw her. I braced myself by grabbing a nearby table, dropping my head and crying out, "NO!" I didn't realize that I had struck the table with my mouth open—so hard that part of my tooth broke off in the table.

This was so unbelievable! I never thought this would happen. I couldn't see this happening just six days after his death. I was in a complete daze.

I read in the Bible and other books of miracles and healing that some were raised from the dead. So, I insisted that the pastor pray and bring my mother back, but it seemed as if she had been gone a while. Her face had no color and her lips were blue. We all stood there in total shock. Since my siblings could not handle making arrangements, I took on that task. I had been numb since I got on the path of preparing my son's Homegoing, so I went ahead on that same path, which was not yet cold.

At this time, I didn't know what to feel. I thought I lost my only son, my daughter is constantly repeating that she was going to be with her brother. Then the rock of the family who I knew would help us get through this tragedy – she was gone, as well.

I was in a daze and angry thinking no matter what I do, I could never please God! Then, I was taunted by the enemy who was saying, "A mother knows how to comfort her own baby." Whenever I heard this, I felt a stabbing feeling inside. The one thing I could remember was when I felt the pain of emptiness for my son, my mom would not cross my mind. The same when I hurt and longed for mom, not one thought of him.

It was all God, as in I Corinthians 10:13:

> *There hath no temptation taken you but such as is common to man: but God is faithful, who will not suffer you to be tempted above that ye are able; but will with the temptation also make a way to escape, that ye may be able to bear it. (KJV)*

We weren't allowed to wear pants, in or out of church. During this time, I found it difficult to put on hosiery or matched socks. I didn't care. I thought about how I'd done all I knew to do, yet my baby's gone. I began to see the church in a whole new light. When I went to church, my skirts were long, tops were buttoned up or zipped up, with long sleeves. So, looking at me, people would take a good look from head to toe and feel that I'm okay, I'm handling it. I looked saved but what I discovered is that my clothes were only a disguise or a costume. My outer appearance did not reveal what was really going on. I looked holy, but my heart was dark – I felt nothing. For a while I learned to put on a face.

Still, I had a fifteen-year-old in so much pain who often spoke of suicide. I felt so alone in this journey. I was wondering how could I help her when I didn't understand? Her friends thought they were helping her cope. They drank vodka in an attempt to help her deal with the pain.

I myself, on the other hand, was drinking wine, after I tried to pray and felt nothing. I know it was a direct attack of the enemy. I'd noticed after drinking half a bottle of wine, I would see my son, or what I thought was him, sitting on the floor in my hallway with his back against the wall, knees up, arms across his knees watching every time I passed by. I envisioned patting him on the head. I looked in his face, which displayed a look of disappointment and sadness. I was hiding the drinking from not only my daughter but from everyone else. I got to the point where I'd take a drink before going to church. Even still, no one noticed. But I still went to church, dragging my daughter with me, red-eyed and reeking of alcohol. Then, I heard this scripture within,

I Corinthians 10:21-22:

> *Ye cannot drink the cup of the Lord, and the cup of devils: ye cannot be partakers of the Lord's table, and of the table of devils. Do we provoke the Lord to jealousy? Are we stronger than he? (KJV)*

I couldn't stop and it didn't seem that my daughter wanted to stop, either. She started the day and ended the night in pain and drinking. I noticed that I felt worse leaving than when I came. My soul was crying out for help. I found a sweatshirt of my son's that he wore for three days before his death. His scent was all through that shirt. It smelled like he was there. When my daughter could not sleep, I'd stretch it out over her pillow. When she didn't use it – I did.

One day, I was alone at home. The Holy Spirit came strong within me. All different praise and worship songs came to my mind. As I sang them, that hoodie came to mind. Then I heard the Holy Spirit speak to me, saying, "That hoodie was being used as an idol for comfort." I knew God was a jealous God:

I Corinthians 10:19:

What say I then? That the idol is anything, or that which is offered in sacrifice to idols is anything? (KJV)

I stopped singing and I heard the Lord say, "Take that hoodie and toss it in the dumpster in the parking lot." I could feel God's presence all over me, as if I was offending Him – finding comfort and peace in an object! And also offering it up as comfort to my child! I felt that I hurt Jesus when He left the Holy Ghost to comfort us. I felt as if I was one of them who yelled out, "Crucify Him! Crucify Him!"

I felt a pit in my belly. I quickly put on my shoes, grabbed the hoodie and ran down the stairs so fast I believe I skipped a step or two. Tossing it in the dumpster, I went back feeling really good about what I did. I felt it pleased God. That feeling I hadn't felt in a very long time.

About an hour later, a wave of grief came over me. As I cried, I thought about that hoodie and anxiety came on strong. I asked myself, "What have you done?" I felt myself hugging that hoodie. I ran down those stairs and prepared to dumpster dive. But when I got there, it was empty. I didn't hear the garbage truck at all. I was devastated and now looking for my wine stash.

During this time, my daughter had two suicide attempts. Both times she was on suicide watch in the hospital. She stayed two weeks each time in a locked facility for treatment. I was leaving the hospital after visiting her, when I ran into a sweet church mother. I had visited her church not too long ago.

She asked me, "How are you doing?"

"I'm OK."

She asked, "How are you really doing?"

Again, I said, "I'm good."

She replied, "No, you're not! You're mad at God."

Quickly, I said, "No. God didn't kill him."

She said, "Be honest with yourself. God already knows and He can handle your anger. So, get it out. Yell at Him. Tell Him how you really feel."

I thought to myself, this lady is trying to get me killed. But the more she talked, the anger was burning within me. As she went on, she pulled me to her hugging me, saying, "Try it."

Crying into her shoulder, I thanked her and got in my car and drove straight to the lake on 95th Street to yell at God. I thought, either I'll get answers, or I'll die here at my favorite place. There was something about the lakefront. I could feel God's presence. I got out of the car angry. I thought, yelling at God could cost me my life – maybe I could be struck by lightning, or a gush of water or wind could cause me to fall off the rock into the choppy water. I went to the top of the rock facing east because the closer east I could feel God. I didn't look around me to see if anyone was around – I didn't care. I felt this was between me and God.

I yelled out loudly, "that was my only son!"

"Jesus was my only son." I heard God reply in a soothing calm voice.

I was like, "Oh God, Wow."

Then, I said, "God, he didn't do anything wrong."

God replied, "Neither did my Son."

I continued, "God, he always helped people."

God replied, "So did my Son."

I then cried out, "He died in the streets like a common criminal."

Again, God replied, "So did my Son."

After this encounter all I could do was cry. I returned to the car repenting, dropping my head. After this I felt a need to get away. It was summer, school was out. I felt my daughter also needed a break. So, we went home with my cousin to South Carolina. It was my birthday when we got there. June turned out not to be such a good month to me, because of all the tragedy in June. All these dates were seared in my mind and rehearsed, so as to never forget. But I wanted to forget, because it was hard to just snap out of it.

Starting with June 5th, that's my son's birthday. He died on the 10th. His Homegoing was on the 14th. Mom died on the 16th. Her Homegoing was on the 20th. Fast approaching after that is my birthday on the 27th. I've often thought of how great it would be if we could skip June altogether and just go from May to July.

I laid across the bed at my cousin's house. I heard the Lord instructing me to lay my open palm on the bed and spread my fingers apart.

I said to myself, "OK. I'm looking. I don't see anything different."

Then suddenly, I could hear God say, "You have five fingers."

I'm thinking to myself, "Yea, and...?"

He continued, "You have four fingers together, and your thumb is separate from them. Yet, they are a part of your hand. Your thumb is Tyree and your momma – separate from you, yet still a part of you."

I was so astonished by this revelation that I ran and told this to my cousin and daughter. They both teared up as I shared this with them. It also came to me to wear a ring on my thumb as a reminder of this special covenant. Since I wanted a thumb ring, my cousin and daughter went shopping to make this birthday special. One of the gifts was a thumb ring, which I have now worn over 20 years. Whenever I thought of them, I'd look at my hand. Later, the ring got damaged, but by that time the covenant was in my heart. As with God's covenant, the covenant with my family is forever. I'll never forget.

Psalms 105:8:

He hath remembered his covenant for ever, the word which he commanded to a thousand generations. (KJV)

When my daughter and I returned home from my cousin's, I was told that the pastor was speaking at another church that night. My goddaughter insisted that I go with them. I told them I'd think about it. She was very persistent, so I said yes, because my daughter wanted to be with her friends. I already knew what that meant and wasn't ready to have that fight. I needed help – I felt like I had nothing left to give her.

I had a drink of wine before leaving. When I walked in the door, the Spirit came upon me. I found a seat at the back. I couldn't tell you what that message was about, but I began dancing in the Spirit in a circle.

I could hear the voice of the Lord speaking to me saying, "Go on a twenty-one-day fast, twenty-four hours on and twenty-four hours off for a straight twenty-one days."

All I could say was, "Yes, Lord." As I came to myself, I vowed to start next week.

As I took my seat, God said sharply, "You will start tomorrow!"

I went home that night and marked the calendar with my 'on' and 'off' days for the twenty-one days.

This was a mandated fast – I couldn't break it, though I wanted to. I started the fast with nothing but water. First, God took that taste for wine, the alcohol. He also took the desire to be hurt – beaten, raped, anything to be hurt. I felt I let my son down somehow. So, I felt I should pay the price that hurt feeling left.

I started praying again and I had to accept the hard truth that God brought back to my mind. It was the remembrance of how I taught my kids that as long as they are obedient to me, God will honor it and protect them. I remembered how I instructed them to stay on the block. My son went outside the perimeter, out of my zone of protection. What happened to him was due to his disobedience. My daughter stayed in the zone until she heard what happened to her brother. She ran there in hopes of being shot along with her brother.

Every year my pastor, at that time, would go on a twenty-one day fast. Only taking in water and juice, when needed. I decided to go on the fast with pastor, as well as two others. I asked God if I could, because I had a great need. I was losing my only remaining child to the streets. I needed to rebuild my prayer life, as well as get instructions from God as to how to help my daughter.

I was also taking classes to be a foster mom. The child was waiting for me to finish. She was a family member of my church. The child's aunt had her sister's kids. She wanted to find them good homes. When she asked me if I could take a girl in, I had to help her. After talking it over with my daughter, she agreed.

God blessed and the fast went well. On the day I came off the fast, the agency called saying that my application went through and they wanted to bring her to me that night. I was weak and tired from the fast, so I asked if they could wait until morning. They understood and agreed, although she really wasn't supposed to come for three days.

I got in bed, which seemed to consume me. It felt so good. I was more tired than hungry. I drank a glass of cranberry juice before going to bed. I heard my daughter coming in. I was already nodding off when my daughter came in and climbed into the bed behind me. I could smell the aroma strongly of alcohol and cigarettes.

She leaned over and whispered in my ear, "Momma, I love you and I'm sorry." Then she fell back to the other side of the bed. Immediately, I sat up and turned on the lights. Her appearance shocked me. Her skin was pasty and pale. Her eyes were red.

She began crying as I asked her, "What did you take?"

She constantly repeated, "I can't live without my brother!" she was yelling and crying.

Whenever I asked, "What did you take? Please tell me."

She again repeated, "I can't live without him!"

As I dressed her, I explained to her, "You will not be with him by committing suicide – you will go to hell! What did you take?"

She was slowly drifting off. I didn't want to call the ambulance because she would've been taken to the local hospital. I wanted her to go to Christ Hospital. They were familiar with her issues. They knew her. This would be the time when my car was not running. Also, my phone was out of minutes. I had no house phone. Her friend lived a block and a half away. I ran there and prayed for my daughter and also, that her friend was home. When I reached her friend's house, I saw her car. I banged on the door, and she snatched the door open, as if she ran to it. I told her I needed her to take us to Christ Hospital.

While I was running back down the stairs, she yelled, "Wait, I'll get my shoes."

"Just come to the house. I have to bring her down the stairs", I told her.

By this time, she was in and out of consciousness. I put her coat on her and used the lapel on her coat to get her down the stairs.

It had to be God carrying that dead weight down a flight of stairs. I was in a weakened state since I still hadn't eaten yet from the fast. I thanked God for the strength to do what needed to be done. All I could think was, I have to get her to Christ Hospital.

Again, I asked her, "Wake up! What did you take?"

She was reaching for her pocket but didn't have enough strength to go in her pocket. She mumbled, "Blood pressure pills and vodka." She cried and then passed out. I went into her pocket and pulled out an empty medicine bottle. My blood pressure medicine bottle had been at least a quarter filled – about fifteen pills were left in there.

When we arrived, I jumped out of the barely stopped car and ran in for help. I told them at the ER desk about my daughter and what she took. A gurney was sent out for her. They took her straight to the back.

One of the nurses that went in with her came out to ask me. "Do you know what she took?"

I handed her the bottle. She asked, "Do you how many were in there?"

"Between ten to fifteen, and she took them with vodka." I told her. The nurse took the bottle and returned to the area where they took her.

Meanwhile, I called my pastor, and the mother's prayer group. An hour had passed and I had not heard a word from anyone. I went to the desk several times and received the same answer, "They will come out and talk to you, Ma'am. They're working on your daughter. Let them help her."

Fifteen minutes later, the nurse came out. I ran to her asking, "How is my daughter?"

"They are still working on her."

"Is she alert?" I asked.

She replied, "No. Not yet." Then she returned to the back.

By this time, I was really feeling the results of the fast and not having anything to eat in twenty-one days. I wasn't really hungry – I just wanted coffee and some much-needed energy. I felt that first sip go all the way through me. I found a seat in the corner in the ER waiting room. I began praying and crying out to God. I repented how I had handled my son's death. I pleaded to God to bring my daughter back to me. After a long while, my begging turned to anger. I asked God, "Is this the reward I receive for all my sacrifice over the years?" After crying out, I repented for making that statement. Deep down, I knew God was always with us and I had to stop speaking out of my pain.

While thanking God for bringing her home, I remembered how many attacks of the enemy she had endured over the years. I was believing in God to not only spare her life, but also to heal her broken heart. Give her a desire to live. I loved her so much. I wanted her to find peace with God and love herself.

After two and one-half hours the doctor came out, saying she's stable and awake. But I couldn't come back to see her for another forty minutes. When I was able to see her, she saw me and started to cry. I could see how weak she was. She looked like a wet rag, I assume from sweat with her hair plastered on her face. Her face had a reddish color; her eyes were still red and puffy – what a sight! But to me she looked like a new baby. My heart burst with love and joy to see her – eyes open and talking. I cried when I was told that I could go in. I didn't know what to expect. All I could do was hold her so tight while holding back tears. I told her how much I loved her and needed her. I knew only God could heal her broken heart and take away that pain.

Seeing her awake, I began thinking of her in full rebellion. I was so angry with her. It filled my mind that I was struggling so hard, so how could I help her? I thought of times I'd yell at her to get it together. But how could she? I'm not there myself. I was just as clueless about what to do and how to do it. I just didn't know how I could help her. I heard a firm whisper, "Love on her the more. Love is a powerful weapon against the enemy."

I John 4:18:

There is no fear in love; but perfect love casts out fear, because fear involves punishment, and the one who fears is not perfected in love. (NASB 95)

God began extending me much patience, wisdom and strength to endure her lashing out and irate behavior. I hugged her even tighter, telling her how much I loved her, as she struggled to get away from me. The more she struggled, the tighter I'd hold her. I told her how important she was, how loved she was by not only me, but by many others, as well. I told her how mighty in God she's going to be because the enemy tried from birth to take her out of here. By God's mercy and grace, she was spared yet again.

Thank you, Father! I recall how God filled her with the Holy Spirit at nine-years-old. Later, she backslid. Then God gave me knowledge of what to do – raise her hands and say, "Hallelujah!" with hands still raised, "Hallelujah!" to the wisdom of God, the Holy Ghost within her, God had me to appeal to what was lying dormant within her.

God had me to appeal to her love of music. She always loved music. She'd hear a song one time and then remembered the entire song. She was never a television watcher, but day and night she listened to radio or cassette tapes. She would be going through a wave of sadness, alone in her room crying.

I'd be in my room not far from hers. I'd yell out, "Hey can you sing me two songs, your choice, for one dollar?"

After three minutes of silence, I'd hear her softly say, "Two songs for a dollar? What? Why?"

I responded, "I just need to hear you sing."

"Okay," she said, "and I want my dollar!"

"Okay," I said. "I got you."

She began singing gospel songs. Afterwards, I'd clap and yell, "Yes! Can I have three songs for one dollar?"

She'd laugh and say, "Just like church people – you trying to cheat me. Nawww!"

I replied, "Okay, okay. How about a quarter a song?"

Laughing, she said, "See what I mean?"

Laughing, I said, "How about a dollar a song? Wow, how you go up like that after two songs?"

Laughing, "Okay she said. A dollar per song and I want my money!"

"You got it, but for a dollar a song, I want a long one with runs and everything."

After two songs, she started singing, "Because He Lives." Before finishing the song, I'd hear her cries of praise to God. I left her alone as I prayed to God on her behalf. When I went in to check on her, it was quiet – she was sound asleep, her face still wet with tears. I kissed her, leaving her quietly so as not to wake her. I used this method for over a year. But later after she got used to me asking, I dropped it to a quarter a song without any resistance. I'd offer more and continued to add songs until she felt God.

By this time, she knew what I was doing. I believe she realized how much better she felt afterwards, so she did it. But as far as I knew, she would only sing when I asked and always for pay. But that was alright with me. I could see what God was doing. But while in bed, she kept on earphones.

After my son's death, I took her out of school. They attended the same high school. I didn't know the reason why my son was shot, so I didn't know if the same would happen to her. I was taunted by the enemy, that she was next. Then I thought of what kind of future she would have without an education. My love and concern for her future became stronger than my fears. I sought out several schools. I went to register her in one school, and I noticed what appeared to be blood on the wall in the staircase – at least it looked like blood to me. I couldn't get out of there fast enough! I came across an accelerated school in downtown Chicago. I had to pay, but I didn't care. I felt she would be safe. That's all I could think about. My only concern was, would she be able to keep up with the state of mind she was in. The school was education only – no extras. If she missed two days she would've been kicked out. It was so fast-tracked that she would never have caught up. It was her junior and senior years in one year.

During this time, my son's trial came up. She wanted to go. I got permission from her school so that she could attend. But she had to study several chapters in her books and take a test when she returned to class. She couldn't fail any test. Going to court brought back so many emotions. When she went back to class and took the test, she failed it. She couldn't seem to focus. It would cost an extra hundred dollars to re-test. They would only give one re-test. I went and talked with her teacher and explained the situation. She was allowed to re-test and also was given extra time. The school waived the extra fee. Without needing the extra time, she passed the test!

She ended up graduating with her regular high school diploma at sixteen-years-old. I felt like I cheated her out of a graduation march with her friends, as well as her senior prom. So, I had her prom dress made and created a prom for her. I gave her boyfriend money to make sure she had the best prom ever. I made reservations at the Cité Restaurant in Lake Point Towers on the 94th floor. After dinner, they were to take a horse and carriage ride through the Chicago loop but they decided to hang out instead until it was time for the midnight cruise. It was a midnight prom cruise with others from several schools. I just wanted her to still have some high school experiences. I tried to make up for missing graduation, but I couldn't.

She wanted to go away for college, but I knew she wasn't ready. She was still grieving and being far from home – I couldn't trust it. She ended up attending Malcolm X College. She was still in a very self-destructive mindset. I didn't want to lose her. She wanted to take a year off school to work. But at sixteen, I felt it would be better to continue going to school. Her grades started off good. She was able to get a grant. When she turned seventeen, she got a job at UPS (United Parcel Service). Her grades dropped. She lost the grant, and I had to pay for classes and books. At eighteen, she became a supervisor making what she thought was a lot of money, which was only $1000 per month. She stopped going to school and decided to go into the Air Force to get her degree in Mortuary Science. I didn't want her to go. I didn't want to argue with her about it. So, I went to God in fasting and prayer. I felt I would lose her for sure.

With a major in Mortuary Science and Funeral Service, in my ignorance, I felt that she would be put on the front line where the killing would be. That's where the dead would be.

She took and passed the Air Force entry test. The recruiter said she was twenty pounds overweight. She went on a Slim Fast diet and lost ten pounds. She was to leave in two weeks. I prayed and fasted more, without telling her how I felt. The recruiter sent and paid for her to have a colonic to lose that extra ten pounds – and she did. I thought she would change her mind, but she never swayed. She was excited about going into the Air Force. She always wanted to be a paratrooper jumping from planes.

There was one more week before she was to be shipped off for basic training. She still worked at UPS as a supervisor and, also, safety coach. A couple days before she was to leave, she had an accident at work, tearing ligaments in her thumb. When she talked to the recruiter about the accident and the length of her recovery, he cancelled her departure and took her off the list for the Air Force. I was secretly happy, but sad about how disappointed she was. She was so excited about going into the Air Force. I knew she wasn't ready yet to be away on her own. I knew she would be okay and ready when her relationship with God was repaired. After that great disappointment, she got refocused on school – transferring to East-West University in downtown Chicago.

Pushing past the disappointment of the Air Force, she found another grant and did very well in school. She stayed on the Dean's list and graduated with excellent grades. Afterwards, she got into Warsham School for Mortuary Science. It turned out to be another accelerated program. She also made it onto the Dean's list and graduated at the top of the class. She had many hurdles, but they only seemed to strengthen her.

She returned to God. The first thing she did was ask seven people to fast and pray with her for seven days from morning until 4:00 pm daily. I told her, "You don't have to ask, I'm with you on this fast." She got the other six with no problem and also made a list of seven things she wanted God to do for restoration and deliverance. The last thing on the list was to meet the husband that God had for her before Christmas of that year. God answered all her requests, including meeting the man who was to be her husband before Thanksgiving. Thing is – they had been knowing each other for years, attending the same church. They were friends – our pastor's son.

They married two years later. The children started coming at the end of the first year. Next year, another. The following year, twins were born. Four children later, she went back to school online twice and was inducted into the National Honor Society.

She earned her master's degree in counseling, using her life skills and trauma to help others.

All I can say is, "To God be the glory!"

Lamentation Part 4:
Yet Another Loss

During this time, I had a foster daughter. She was sweet, quiet, as well as overcoming many hurts of her own when losing her own mother. I didn't feel stable enough to adopt her. I really wanted to. I loved her as my own. I was pushed by the agency to adopt her. I moved a few times. I was threatened by the agency that they would take her if I didn't get stabilized.

She became very comfortable living with us. She was like a little sister and a daughter to us. But I was suffering from PTSD (Post Traumatic Stress Disorder). Strong fear would come upon me when she was out playing. Her friends had bikes in the neighborhood. She wanted one, too. So, I got her one. She'd ride it in the apartment complex where we lived. If ten minutes passed and I didn't see her coming around the corner, I went looking for her in full panic mode, heart pounding. When I saw her, I asked what happened. Why didn't she come back? She said they got off the bikes to play on the playground in the back of the complex. I panicked that something happened to her. I felt very selfish at this point – realizing this is no way to raise a child. I loved her so much I was very over-protective. I wanted her to enjoy her childhood, in a normal home.

I moved to Indiana closer to my church. I wasn't thinking that I crossed state lines with her and that was not permitted. I was momma to her; she was my daughter, and I just moved with her.

At this time, she was attending school in Chicago. We rode the city bus daily. While she was in school, I would use that time for appointments and visiting. When the social worker was informed, I received a call. She insisted that she had to move the child because I was in another state. I asked her for time to find another apartment in Chicago. I also asked if the child could be placed in an agency in Indiana? I was told, no – she couldn't authorize that. Later, I found out that the social worker could have transferred her to an agency in Indiana.

When I called her with the information to transfer the case, she excitedly informed me that she found another home for my foster child. The social worker continued describing the two parents. They were an elderly couple who had already adopted two girls around the age of my foster child. When I thought about that dynamic family with a mom, dad and sisters, I felt that maybe this would be best for her.

It was very difficult to let her go. Grief hit me again; this was another loss. The pain of losing her became bearable when I thought of how it could benefit her. At this time, my daughter and I struggled – our emotions were all over the place. This was a chance for the child to be in a stable home. But my heart was broken because she didn't want to go. I tried to convince her that this would be best for her. I told her social worker that I didn't want her bounced around in the system. I told the child that I would visit as often as I'm allowed by her new parents.

She was taken to join her new family a week before her birthday. Sad as this was, I took many gifts which included a photo album of her entire time with us. This included the schools she went to, pictures of her friends, clothing and trinkets. I also included gifts for her new sisters. Shortly after her birthday, she ran away. She went to my sister's house, once my family home where she had been many times. That really broke my heart. To me, that meant that she wasn't adjusting well. I talked with her; then I returned her to her home. Then I was informed that I had a restraining order against me. This prevented me from coming within feet of her home, school and playground, or I would be arrested. That was awful news. We were all transitioning and this really added sadness to the situation.

I remember how she continued to call me "momma" as I was leaving her on her birthday. I would correct her by saying, "Momma is the one who cares about you and takes care of you. Now, you can think of me as your 'godmother'. But your new foster parents are now your momma and daddy."

We missed her very much. I would often drive by her house and the surrounding area hoping to see her. A few times I would see her in the park that wasn't far from her home, laughing and playing with her sisters. It was good to see her laughing again. I was careful not to let her see me. I was looking forward to her contacting us following her eighteenth birthday. When I didn't hear from her, I asked her aunt, from the church we used to attend, how she was doing. I found out she was married with two little boys and expecting her third child – a girl.

My daughter and I connected with her and met her family. She was a good mother who cared for her family. We connected online, but this relationship is not nearly what I wanted with her and her family. God is real. He will do it for you, as well.

When Depression Challenged My Faith

Psalms 23:4

> *Even though I walk through the valley of the shadow of death, I fear no evil; for though art with me; thy rod and thy staff they comfort me. (NASB 95)*

In 2019, I discovered that one of the side effects of at least one of my medications was damaging my kidneys. I kept up with my GFR number, which was the Glomerular Filtration Rate. This is a measure of how well your kidneys are filtering blood. This is the primary way to measure kidney function.

I remembered how for three years I took my father to dialysis and saw how drained he was afterwards. I wanted no part of that for myself. I watched the quality of life, or lack thereof, literally drain from his body. I absolutely wanted no part of this treatment.

I shared this with my pastor of 'Faith Hope & Charity'. I told him about my medication and what damage it was doing to my kidneys. I also told him about not wanting dialysis. I had been told that I was in kidney disease. Prior to this conversation, I prayed, asking what I could do about this situation. God told me to get permission from the pastor to put all my meds on the altar. I shared with my pastor what God shared with me. I asked if I could leave a bag of my medication on the altar. He replied, "Yes, I will be praying over them with you." I placed the bag of medication on the altar between the podium and a floral arrangement, so it was not exposed to the congregation. Originally, I was only going to leave them there for a week, but they were there for a month. I would only take out the meds I needed for each week.

That following month I had an appointment at the 'Heart Failure Clinic (HFC).' It was the clinic that monitored my blood every three months. They also checked my meds and organ functions. I kept track of my numbers, where I was, and also where the numbers should be. Most times, if you don't ask questions, you won't get answers. Only your sodium content and your water weight gain were discussed. With this visit, I was told I was even farther into kidney disease. I asked what my GFR was? It was down to thirty-five at that time. I was told it should've been sixty or higher.

During this time my pastor took on a fatherly role and asked me, "Can you go? Are you able to go?" I closed my eyes and dropped my head ashamed. I replied. "Not too much, maybe once or twice a day." Because I was dehydrated, I was told not to consume more than 1½ liters of fluid per day. This was hard to do, but I did it. I was doing as I was told by the nurses and doctors in the Heart Failure Clinic. Nevertheless, I was often in and out of the hospital as a patient.

I was already suffering from PTSD (Post Traumatic Stress Disorder) and also depression. This situation seemed to make things worse. That news put me in an even darker place. My doctor suggested that I enroll in a program at Little Company of Mary Hospital for depression. The program was for five weeks, 7½ hours a day, Monday through Friday.

I shared the intensity of this program with my daughter and her husband. They both agreed to support me by giving me fare to get there and many times, they picked me up and took me home or to their house, when I had a hard time in therapy.

Two weeks into the program, I shared with my pastor's wife, and she shared with my pastor (because I was ashamed to tell him) that I was in this program. There was a stigma; if a saint was really saved, they didn't suffer depression or any mental illness. If you did, then you lacked faith and didn't trust God. So, I was not eager to tell anyone. I was so grateful for all the love and support I received during this time. When I started, the doctor put me on medication which seemed to have drifted me into a darker space – down the 'rabbit hole' is what they called it. Yes, I loved God and was living for Him with all I knew. But with the horrors of my past, the sickness of my present seemed to have held me hostage. I wore a mask for so long that no one knew what was going on, on the inside. All the while, I was looking to God for deliverance.

The hospital group sessions were so intense. I was coping with my issues and now the group issue was added. I began noticing how I had to push myself to attend church, because I was in such a weird space. The inside was now showing on the outside. I didn't realize it at the time, but when I entered the darkness, I carried a blank look on my face and spoke very little. It was as if the lights were on, but no one was home. I felt distant and alone.

One Sunday morning, I sat alone trying to focus on the preached word, feeling very paranoid and aware that this was new behavior. I felt alone in every room, no matter how many people were there. To me it was a dark and extremely weird space. Then I felt a close presence of peace. Looking up, it was my daughter. Normally, she sat on the other side of the sanctuary. She came over and sat beside me, and two of her kids followed her and sat on her other side. It was as if she could feel my struggles. She sat close and took hold of my hand. As she did so, I felt as if that stronghold that had me bound was broken. The darkness, as well as the coldness within was lifted and warmed my heart. I was able to focus on the preacher's word.

Later, I asked her, "What made you come sit with me?"

She replied, "God told her to come – that I needed her."

I really did, but at the time I didn't know what I needed until she sat beside me and took my hand.

I really believe it was the medication that was prescribed when I got into the program at Little Company of Mary Hospital. In different programs for those suffering with mental illness, I've seen people staring off into space, slobbering, nose running – totally weird behavior. I was so paranoid about this happening to me. I found myself constantly checking my nose and mouth to make sure I wasn't slobbering or running. Now wiping and checking ended up taking root as a new behavior of mine. I was very conscious of paranoia and the meds. I thought I didn't have this problem before. I'm getting worse, not better, and I struggled not to allow this to happen to me.

I would get to church early just to sit in the back of the sanctuary, hopefully, to be able to meditate. This was one of the things taught in the class at the hospital. On Sunday mornings, my son-in-love was over the music. After Sunday School was over, he'd play praise and worship music in the sanctuary between services; it lasted thirty minutes. Sitting and meditating on God really helped me to be in the moment. I could not do this without God, I thought.

One Sunday morning, as pastor was sharing the word of God, he looked out over the congregation. I dropped my head as he looked my way. I did not expect what he did next. He came down from the pulpit and grabbed the bottle of oil (olive oil used for blessing, healing and deliverance). He came right to me, while pouring the oil on his hand. I wanted to run – my mind was racing. He cupped my forehead, praying and rebuking that spirit that was upon me. He also spoke about health and healing. I could feel the power of God upon me.

The following week I had an appointment with the Heart Failure Clinic. I was told that my kidney function was two points from the normal range! The doctor was amazed due to my age and medical history. I shared the news with my pastor of how God and the power of prayer was healing my kidneys.

Yet again, the enemy didn't want to loosen his hold on me. I began dragging my leg which had become too painful to lift or bend. The doctor told me about the lower disk in my spine was degenerating. Therefore, I need surgery. Immediately, I responded, "No!" to the surgery. Now this was years ago and I'm walking fine without that surgery. I thank God for the power of prayer.

My daughter and son-in-love were very supportive every step of the way. Whatever was needed, they were there. When I look back, I thank God that I did not face this journey alone. Many in my group did not have a support system, and they were given mentors.

I continued the group sessions. I was called out of one session to see the doctor who prescribed the meds for depression. I explained how I was in a dark place very often and he changed my prescription. I was very relieved. Not only did the first meds have me in a dark and lonely space, but I also gained some weight – which I hated.

I started the new meds the following day. Right away, after taking the new meds, I noticed my mouth was extremely dry and it was difficult to swallow. There was little to no saliva. But I didn't complain because I began to lose that extra weight. I had no appetite for food, but I desired lots of water. I had very little food or snacks and because I was losing the extra weight, I remained silent. Then, my body began to retain the extra fluid. That caused a problem with my congestive heart failure. My weight began to elevate again and I knew that was a huge problem and not healthy at all.

I made an appointment to see the doctor early to share with him the problem I was experiencing on my third medication. I was so discouraged that the counselor encouraged me, "Everyone's body is different and they're looking for your perfect fit. Just relax. It won't be long – he'll get it. You'll be okay. But if it's a problem, don't sit on it – call the doctor."

I often heard with psychotropic drugs, that one of the side effects would be suicidal thoughts. I thought that was a myth or impossible. I felt that if you were in a suicidal frame of mind, you'd possibly have those thoughts, but I wasn't. After three days of taking the new meds, I was home alone and crying for no apparent reason. Then I began to hear words as clearly as if it was spoken in my ear: "There is no hope or help for you. This is the third medication. You're wasting your time. Your family is tired.

Just give up! Just take the whole bottle now! You and everyone would be better off!"

I wrestled with that attack of the enemy for over an hour and cried all the more knowing how that would not only hurt God, but my family, as well. Still, I entertained the fact that my family was tired. Then I was thinking that suicide was a sin, and the body didn't belong to me. Then I could hear God's word as it was also spoken to me.

I Corinthians 6:19-20:

What? Know ye not that your body is the temple of the Holy Ghost which is in you, which ye have of God, and ye are not your own?

For ye are bought with a price: therefore glorify God in your body, and in your spirit, which are God's. (KJV)

One day during these struggles, I received a call from my daughter. She noticed that I was crying and couldn't stop.

She repeatedly asked, "What is wrong?" I was pondering whether I should tell her.

She kept asking, "What's the matter? Are you in pain?"

Softly, I said, "I'm not in pain." Then, I shared with her out of fear of how that spirit had a hold on me. It was attempting to convince me of this horrible deed. She and the grandchildren were already in the car. I could hear them laughing and talking. She told me, "I'm on my way to pick you up."

I pleaded with her not to come, because I couldn't stop crying. I didn't want to upset the kids or have them see me that way. She wouldn't take 'No' for an answer.

It seemed like minutes later that she called back, "I'm here. Come on down."

I hesitated. She said, "Don't make me take these babies out of the car seats and come up to get you."

Deep down, I knew I should go. I went down to the car without looking at the kids. I said, "Hey y'all." That evil voice had started to be convincing. Thank God, the kids didn't notice anything. They all yelled out, "Hi Grandma!" as they continued to play. I could not shut off the water works – I continued to weep. I was thinking – I'm in trouble, God. So, I sat in the car pleading to God. It came to me to Google that and see what comes up. What came up was so perfect. God heard me.

The words to say to God are in Psalm 31:9:

> *Have mercy upon me, O Lord, for I am in trouble: mine eye is consumed with grief, yea, my soul and my belly. (KJV)*

Through the turmoil, I read and repeated this scripture, exchanging all that I was experiencing in my mind while wrestling with the evil spirit.

My daughter could tell that I didn't want to talk. She had praise and worship music on the radio as she drove in silence. She drove into the store parking lot, got out and went into the grocery store. My phone rang. I looked at the Caller ID. It was the pharmacist from Walgreens calling about the new medication. She asked to speak to me. I responded, "This is she." Still whimpering. She said she was checking on me because I was yet on another new medication. I thought the call was unusual since no one had called the other two times. But I thank God for that follow-up call. I continued weeping as I explained what I was feeling, as well as the voice and the words spoken to me. She asked if I were alone and to call 911. She said that I must be experiencing an allergic reaction to that medication. I explained to her that I was not alone. That my daughter came to get me. She told me to stop taking that medication and contact my doctor.

The doctor said he would send in another prescription. At this point, I really didn't think that anything would help. I was so skeptical about trying another drug that I was beginning to feel like a lab rat. I saw it as a toss-up between the PTSD and depression versus another unfit medication.

To my surprise, the new medication was a good fit. I felt normal without side effects. There were no ups and downs. I had better control of my thoughts and feelings that seemed to come along with the PTSD and depression than I had been experiencing for years.

I Peter 5:6-8:

> *Humble yourselves therefore under the mighty hand of God, that he may exalt you in due time: Casting all your care upon him; for he careth for you. Be sober, be vigilant; because your adversary the devil, as a roaring lion, walketh about, seeking whom he may devour: (KJV)*

I came to realize that he wasn't a lion that could tear into your flesh, but a loud noise of confusion that would have you believe he could.

Enduring this whole process made me realize how many are taking medication for depression or many of the other mental illnesses. They are either staying in an unrecognizable state of mind or just giving up altogether. Returning to the darkness within that became so familiar to them. Or by taking no medication and returning to their old state of mind. It took four different medication changes to find that good fit for me.

And this is another way the enemy works, as well, deceiving many. I feel so normal now. Even better than my old self. Very normal. It could be so easy for me to say, 'I'm fine'. I don't feel anything. No dizziness, no extra appetite, no voices, no crying for no reason. So does that mean I'm healed, and I really don't need them. No! It means the medication is a good fit and it's working. Now I'm back focusing on my health. My kidney function has improved. With my medical history, the nurses were very impressed with my test numbers, which turned out to be above normal.

To God be the glory! Hallelujah!

Because I was helped, I was able to get back in my place of encouraging others – helping others where I could, with resources and warm loving hugs and prayers.

Wrinkled Sheets

As we attempt to fulfill a purposed-filled life, we experience many challenges, choices, sacrifices, and denials that are designed to humble the flesh and spirit.

When something occurs which seems to be somewhat impossible, I'm forced to answer the questions of the Serenity Prayer. It instantly just makes so much sense to me:

"God grant me the serenity to accept the things I cannot change, the courage to change things I can, and the wisdom to know the difference."

This is what came to mind – "Wrinkled Sheets". Why wrinkled sheets? We were not in our great grandparent's day when ironing sheets was a must. But I'm not speaking of that kind of wrinkles. But of wrinkles that interrupt your day as night comes and throughout the night.

Let me explain, I was recovering from rotator cuff surgery. There were many restrictions to my healing – such as no pulling, no stretching, nor lifting anything over five pounds. All these restrictions described changing the sheets on my bed, at least the fitted sheet. That has to be stretched to make it smooth.

Well, due to complications during surgery, my daughter insisted I stay with her family for the first two months. At this time, I felt capable enough to go home alone and care for myself. I had prepared twenty-six frozen meals. I learned to bathe and dress. Sidestepping a potential complication, I learned how to prevent frustrations such as avoiding wearing clothes that I knew would be a challenge taking off. Or wanting something to eat other than my prepared meals. I cooked eggs and breakfast meals in the microwave to avoid lifting heavy pots and pans. Piece of cake, I thought. Then comes that thing that literally knocks you off your square! That difficult thing that never crossed your mind.

I needed to change my sheets. I stood there frozen. Thinking of everything I'm NOT to do, but ... I needed to change my sheets. I pushed it out of my mind, till one day it had to be done. So, using my left hand I got them off the bed and washed and dried them. These were my favorite sheets, so I wanted them back on the bed. Pure white cotton sheets, smooth and comfortable but coming out of the dryer, it was a big balled up mess! Now knowing what would press these sheets out was the deep pockets and corner stretch over the mattress. Yes – nice and smooth, but this I saw was impossible to accomplish. I realized everything I needed to do to get this sheet on the bed were things I was NOT to do. I reached out to a few people who promised to come but they couldn't, so I had to figure it out. Sleeping on a bare mattress was out of the question. So, I folded them over and put them away. Now what to do? Ok, I thought I'll put a flat sheet over the mattress. I tucked it under the best I could with my left hand. No top sheet, which I've never done but the bed was made. Thank God! I thought.

Have you ever had little things that bothered you so much, they kept you awake at night? And they took up so much residency in your mind, you couldn't think of anything else the closer it got to evening. I did not see this coming. How happy I was to just figure it out, to sleep in a fresh bed. I discovered after getting in bed and scooting over without the support of my right arm that by not being tucked in well, the sheet went with you! I got right up to straighten and tuck the sheet after seeing how wrinkled it was with part of the mattress showing!

I fixed it and returned to bed – only for it to happen again. Then, it started bothering me that there was no top sheet. I just wanted to scream! I never knew this about myself. How everything had to be just so. I had a tantrum like a spoiled brat. It had to be smooth fitted sheet, top flat sheet with comforter – in that designed order – where you can toss and turn all night and everything stays in place.

I couldn't get help at that time. Then it came to me – this little thing should not have this much power over me. With restless nights and frustrating days, I'd stand before going to bed knowing what chaos was awaiting under that comforter. I just stood there thinking, how could this take me hostage this way?

Thinking there had to be a lesson in this, I asked God, "what are you trying to show me?" Again, I answered all the questions of the Serenity Prayer. Can I make it better? No. Can I tuck the sheet under to stay or lift the mattress cuffing under it? No. So to get through this sheet situation, I had to stop focusing on something I could not change. I thought – this was the reason I was not able to get help. And we should not cower down when faced with unexpected challenges.

Philippians 4:12-13:

> *I know both how to be abased and I know how to abound: everywhere and in all things I am instructed both to be full and to be hungry, both to abound and suffer need. I can do all things through Christ which strengtheneth me. (KJV)*

This situation has taught me that we must adapt to every and whatever situation we may find ourselves in. Just roll with it. Real-life things happen beyond our control. On this journey of purpose, we have no idea what's ahead.

Song of Solomon 2:15b:

...the little foxes that are ruining the vineyards, while our vineyards are in blossom. (NASB)

Whenever we may have a problem or a very difficult encounter to adapt to, preparing ourselves with prayer can help. Especially, if your reactions sometimes do not match the situation or there was something you were missing. In the case of the wrinkled sheets, I found this to be so.

Now I slept that way for over two months. I finally came to a place where I didn't get up to fix it. I tried very hard to ignore it. I stopped complaining about it. Never thought the day would come when I was able to lay there and it does not bother me.

Finally, the day came, and my fave sheets were put on right, well, MY WAY of right –fitted sheet, flat sheet, and comforter. I remember how excited I was going to bed that night. I texted my daughter right away. Hugs, kisses every time I get in bed. I turned over and the bottom sheet stayed in place! That felt so amazing! I thought about how upset I was to sleep that other way for that long.

With everything that I was NOT to do, I rehearsed "The Serenity Prayer" and Paul's words. I constantly asked myself, could I have done anything differently? If so, why hesitate, just do it. If I couldn't change the narrative of the situation – make friends with it. Continue as if it's the norm. As Paul reminisced, I've had it good, and I remember that! Yes, the bad was very bad and I got through that. I remembered a time when I was so very hungry, also thought of when I couldn't take another bite. I had to learn these lessons.

Now when facing difficult, frustrating situations, I've learned to breathe and relax, not complain. I have learned not to focus on what I am not able to do but rejoice on those challenging tasks I am able to complete, even if I have to change the way it's normally done. I can only give glory to the Holy Spirit for the leading of my given path. Now I can clearly see, having gone through it, some of the lessons in the valley. When frustrated, ask the Holy Spirit to show you how to fix it. More importantly, don't give in to the frustrations, especially without any effort of correcting it. Now at some point, even after you make an attempt to make it better, you must communicate with the Father about it. It may be better for you to be content in that state of being. Remember, it's only for a season -- the troubles, frustrations, the low in spirit. As Paul did, he learned to be content. Is that easy? Absolutely NOT! When you have had it your way, your happy place being content, everything can change suddenly at any given time. When this happens, do we fold sitting under a juniper tree as Elijah, waiting to die (I King 19:4)? It's the simple things we see as boulders when they are simply pebbles.

I came to a point where I simply did not care. Taking on the Spirit -- I don't care! I got in bed wrinkles and all and didn't try to fix it. I wasn't bothered by it in the least. I had the attitude

– it is what it is. Was I happy about this? Absolutely NOT! But I felt if God wanted it fixed, it would've been done. I checked my attitude. Stop feeling sorry for myself; stop asking myself -- why didn't God send help? He sees and knows what I'm going through.

I then came to a place of feeling and hearing the cries of those that had no bed. They would've fared well in my situation. I had a roof over my head, clean linen, and food at my disposal. I started thinking my complaint, frustrations, anger was someone's prayer of hope. No matter how or in what state it was – we got there. Prayer was answered. I began repenting, weeping, and thanking God because it could have been me. By this time, this no longer seemed like a struggle. When I stopped fighting and complaining and completely surrendered my will and way, help came to put the sheets on.

Thank God! I felt I passed this test, this lesson. Almost three weeks later, I traveled out of town, visiting. The first night when I went to bed, I pulled back the comforter only to see a soft single fitted sheet that was too large for the mattress, looking like ocean waves, with no top sheet. I knew that I did not share this battle with anyone. I've stayed at this place before and the sheets were not this way. It was tight fitted sheets with matching top sheet and comforter. At this point, I knew I conquered this battle. I passed. I really knew I had the victory when I pulled back the comforter, without hesitation, with no top sheet, got in bed, snuggled in the deep waves of the sheets, laughed and went to sleep … and slept well without a second thought!

Well, my wrinkled sheets may not seem like a big deal to many. But your Big Deal, your Boulder may not affect me, nor mine affect you. Matter of fact, this chapter or even the title may have caused you to laugh. But God knows each of His children, as well as what we must possess to be not only fit for His kingdom but also possess the character to work in His vineyard interacting with the lost and suffering souls. It would take the likeness and true character of God not to react to the smallest events in our own lives. Events that at one time literally knocked us off our square and totally out of character.

Epilogue

Currently, I'm still seeing a therapist on Zoom and doing better. I'm enjoying my grandchildren as they grow into their own selves. I can say when I look back over my life that God has been good to me. This last trial was meant to destroy me, but God kept my mind through it all. I am so grateful to God for all He has done and all He continues to do.

I have even greater compassion for the homeless. I've been homeless several times. I often pray for resources for them, and I take supplies when our group goes out. I also go out with my daughter and the grandkids on Sunday mornings before church. At times, we take coffee and breakfast sandwiches. I joined the 88SAINT (773-887-2468) prayer line that was established in 2016. I joined in 2020-2021. My prayer is every Wednesday at noon. I pray that someone finds faith, comfort and peace throughout these chapters.

Luke 18:1:

And he spake a parable unto them to this end, that men ought always to pray, and not to faint (KJV)

www.ingramcontent.com/pod-product-compliance
Lightning Source LLC
Chambersburg PA
CBHW021106130626
46554CB00002B/561

* 9 7 8 1 9 6 4 0 6 1 3 9 9 *